THE BEST
POLITICAL CARTOONS
OF THE YEAR
2005
EDITION

Edited by
Daryl Cagle and
Brian Fairrington

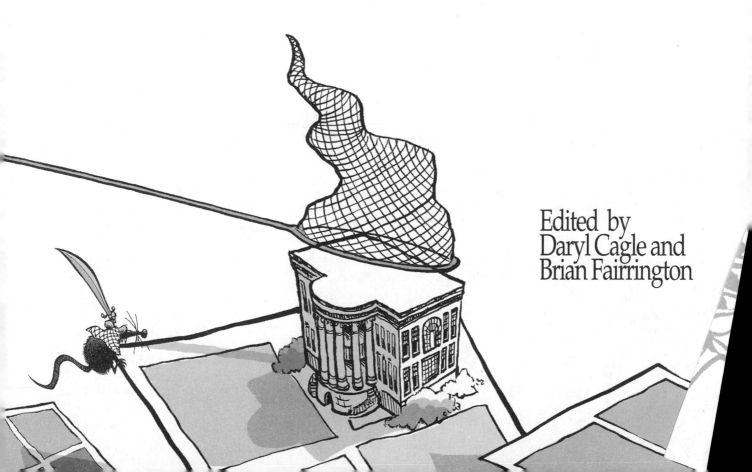

Dedication

This book is dedicated to the many editorial cartoonists who have recently lost their jobs as our art form suffers a slow decline.

The Best Political Cartoons of the Year, 2005 Edition

Daryl Cagle, Cartoonist-Editor, Cover

Brian Fairrington, Cartoonist-Editor, Back Cover and Inside Front Cover

Susan Cagle, Copy Editor

Greg Wiegand, Associate Publisher, Que Publishing

Laura Norman, Acquisitions Editor, Que Publishing

International Standard Book Number: 0-7897-3350-1
Library of Congress Catalog Card Number: 2004112819
Printed in the United States of America
First Printing: December 2004
07 06 05   3 2

Trademarks

Warning and Disclaimer

Bulk Sales.

Que Publishing offers excellent discounts on this book when ordered in quantity for bulk purchases or special sales. For more information, please contact:
    U.S. Corporate and Government Sales
    1-800-382-3419
    corpsales@pearsontechgroup.com

For sales outside the United States, please contact
    International Sales
    international@pearsoned.com

800 East 96th Street
Indianapolis, Indiana 46240

THE BEST POLITICAL CARTOONS OF THE YEAR 2005

Table of Contents

About This Book

We run the colossal web site, cagle.com that features all the newest and best political cartoons by all the best cartoonists. The most popular feature on our site is our annual retrospective of the best cartoons of the year. Our fans have been writing, begging us to do a book for years – and with so much crazy news this year, we knew we had to do it now. So here it is!

The *Best Political Cartoons of the Year*, 2005 Edition is really about the best cartoons of 2004, but since our book comes out in 2005, we call it the 2005 edition. The cartoonists in this book are the best in the world. There are no amateurs or wannabes here, as you'll see in other "best of" books: These guys are the crème de la crème. Every cartoonist here is a regular contributor to our web site, where we post dated archives of all of their cartoons. Want to contact one of them? Just visit our site for every cartoonist's e-mail address.

Our book is organized like our web site, with a chapter on each major topic of the year. This was an important year with the presidential campaign, war in Iraq, and terror: Terrorists attacked a Russian school, killing scores of children, and terrorists bombed trains in Madrid, influencing Spain's presidential election. But there was more to 2004 than war, terror and politics. We saw the Olympics in Athens and the Red Sox won the World Series for the first time in 86 years. A bizarre series of killer hurricanes battered Florida and the Gulf Coast. Bill Clinton came back into the public spotlight with both a book tour and heart surgery. Noteworthy icons passed from the scene, from Ronald Reagan to Ray Charles, Rodney Dangerfield and Yasser Arafat. Martha Stewart went to jail. This was a Renaissance year for cartoonists.

As most cartoonists are liberal, this book may have a liberal slant, but we have no partisan bias in selecting the cartoons. The best cartoons are simply the best cartoons, whether from the right or from the left. The cartoonists have a broad range of styles and perspectives, and their cartoons run the gamut from serious commentary to silly jokes. Editorial cartoons are an art form that chronicles history and reflects the attitudes of the public with a depth that can't be achieved in words alone. We see this book as an historical document, a snapshot in time that captures the attitudes and opinions of America in 2004.

And after reviewing this year in cartoons, visit our web site for the best cartoons of the day, every day – cagle.com. New cartoon history is being made all the time.

Daryl Cagle

About the Editor-Cartoonists

Daryl Cagle

Daryl is the daily editorial cartoonist for the Microsoft Network's commentary site, *Slate*. With over three million regular, unique users each month, Daryl's editorial cartoon site with Microsoft (cagle.slate.msn.com) is the most popular cartoon web site, of any kind, on the Internet. It is also the most widely used education site in social studies classrooms around the world.

For the past twenty eight years, Daryl has been one of America's most prolific cartoonists. Raised in California, Daryl went to college at UC Santa Barbara, then moved to New York City where he worked for ten years with *Jim Henson's Muppets*, illustrating scores of books, magazines, calendars and all manner of products.

In 2001, Daryl started a new syndicate, *Cagle Cartoons, Inc.* (http://caglecartoons.com), which distributes the cartoons of twenty editorial cartoonists and columnists to over eight hundred newspapers in the USA, Canada and Latin America. Daryl is a past president of the National Cartoonists Society. He has been married for twenty years and has two lovely children, Susan and Michael.

Brian Fairrington

Brian is one of the most accomplished young cartoonists in the country. While at Arizona State University, Brian won the John Locher Memorial Award from the Association of American Editorial Cartoonists. He also won the Charles M. Schulz Award from the Scripps Howard Foundation as the best college cartoonist. Since turning pro, Brian has gathered a bunch of new, glittering, cartooning trophies.

Brian works as a contributing political cartoonist for the *Arizona Republic*, his cartoons are nationally syndicated to over 800 newspapers by *Cagle Cartoons* (www.caglecartoons.com). Fox News named a cartoon of his as "number one" in their best cartoons of the year countdown.

Brian is married to Stacey Heywood and they have two children, Chase 4, Hayden 2, and a third baby due in the spring of 2005. Besides drawing, his hobbies include performing turn of the century Russian dental procedures on abandoned mountain gorillas and mounting stuffed brown squirrels on pieces of dry driftwood.

Cagle portrait by Taylor Jones, Fairrington Portrait by Fairrington

We Want to Hear from You!

As the reader of this book, you are our most important critic and commentator. We value your opinion and want to know what we're doing right, what we could do better, what areas you'd like to see us publish in, and any other words of wisdom you're willing to pass our way.

As an associate publisher for Que Publishing, I welcome your comments. You can email or write me directly to let me know what you did or didn't like about this book—as well as what we can do to make our books better.

When you write, please be sure to include this book's title and author as well as your name, email address, and phone number. I will carefully review your comments and share them with the author and editors who worked on the book.

Email: feedback@quepublishing.com

Mail: Greg Wiegand
   Associate Publisher
   Que Publishing
   800 East 96th Street
   Indianapolis, IN 46240 USA

For more information about this book or another Que Publishing title, visit our Web site at www.quepublishing.com. Type the ISBN (excluding hyphens) or the title of a book in the Search field to find the page you're looking for.

Foreword by Howard Dean

Taylor Jones - 2004

©2004 Tribune Media Services, Inc.

Dean portrait by Taylor Jones

A recent survey of Americans under 30 years old showed that a majority got their news from the Internet and *The Daily Show* with Jon Stewart. We should not be surprised.

Humor has been used for well over a hundred years in American newspapers in the form of political cartoons. One well-thought-out cartoon can say more about hypocrisy, courage, venality, honor, foolishness or compassion than so many articles. Political cartoons can be scathing, pointed and enlightening. They are commentary—and they are news.

I enjoy writing a column about policy and politics for *Cagle Cartoons* once a week. But, I bet that the other columnists and I have little impact compared to the poignant, thought-provoking cartoons that are distributed by Cagle each week. There is something about a really good cartoon that says it all—quickly and concisely.

-Gov. Howard Dean, M.D.

Ronald Reagan Passes
by Michael Reagan

Politics can be a serious business. Millions of words are written and spoken about the goings-on in Washington, D.C. and other political capitals. But what a political cartoonist does with a sketch and just a few words is remarkable, often doing more than all of the talking heads and columns of type to crystallize our understanding of an issue or person.

During his political life, my father was portrayed in a variety of ways by many different cartoonists. It's no secret that most political cartoonists are liberal, and many did not agree with his politics.

When Dad passed away last year, most of those same artists chose to focus on his accomplishments. The cartoons were moving, heartfelt memorials, showing appreciation and honor for my dad. I suppose I could say that is somewhat ironic, but I think it serves as a testament to the talent, understanding and passion of the cartoonists featured here. Cartoonists do love irony.

As I wrote after Dad's funeral, America's love and regard for him has sustained me and my family in these difficult months. After all, Dad had not been in the public eye for ten years but during that time, which Nancy called "the long goodbye," it now appears that the love for him continued to grow. People came to understand the respect he showed for the office of president, the respect he showed for each and every one of us and the optimistic vision he had for America's future— that we could always do better. His message was always hopeful; it inspired us and continues to inspire us.

All of you made it so much easier for us to get through those emotion-filled days we spent in the public eye and under the glare of the TV lights. You helped turn what could have been a grief-filled experience into a week-long, awe-inspiring series of moments.

Thank you, America. My dad loved you, and so do we. You are the finest, most decent and loving people in the world.

Michael Reagan

2

STEVE BENSON, Arizona Republic

HEAVEN IS NOW Reagan Country

BRIAN FAIRRINGTON
Cagle Cartoons

3

MOURNING IN AMERICA

MIKE THOMPSON
Detroit Free Press

DARYL CAGLE
Slate.com

DAVID HORSEY
Seattle Post Intelligencer

4

MIKE LESTER, Rome News-Tribune, GA

DOUG MARLETTE, Tallahassee Democrat, FL

MICHAEL RAMIREZ, Los Angeles Times

STEVE BREEN, San Diego Union-Tribune

GARY MARKSTEIN,
Milwaukee Journal-Sentinel

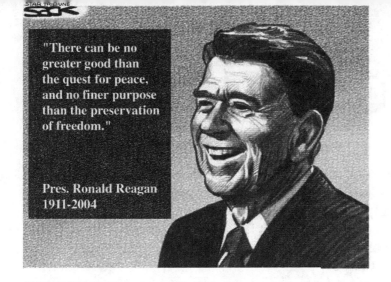

"There can be no greater good than the quest for peace, and no finer purpose than the preservation of freedom."

Pres. Ronald Reagan
1911-2004

STEVE SACK, Minneapolis Star-Tribune

HENRY PAYNE, Detroit News

Janet's Boob

The year 2004 kicked off with a bang, or more appropriately, a boob, when part of Janet Jackson's anatomy took center stage at the Super Bowl half time show. Singer Justin Timberlake declared, "I'm gonna get you naked by the end of this song," and "accidently" ripped off a strange bit of Janet's costume, revealing a star shaped metal pasty on her breast. The network quickly cut away and didn't mention the incident, which was replayed more than any other TV moment in the history of TiVo. At a press conference, Timberlake complained of a "wardrobe malfunction," a term that entered the national lexicon. What followed was a firestorm of controversy over decency standards on television, prompting the FCC to turn up the heat on other shows with questionable programming.

In an election year, with a war in Iraq, genocide in Africa, and the Olympics, the most popular cartoons were the ones about Janet's breast.

MIKE LESTER
Rome News-Tribune, GA

JOHN DARKOW, Columbia Daily Tribune

CAL GRONDAHL, Utah Standard-Examiner

DWANE POWELL, Raliegh News & Observer

ROB ROGERS, Pittsburgh Post-Gazette

JEFF STAHLER, Cincinnati Post

JEFF STAHLER, Cincinnati Post

JOHN TREVER, Albuquerque Journal

MIKE LESTER,
Rome News-Tribune, GA

CAMERON CARDOW, Ottawa Citizen

STEVE KELLEY, New Orleans Times-Picayune

DARYL CAGLE, Slate.com

STEVE KELLEY,
New Orleans Times-Picayune

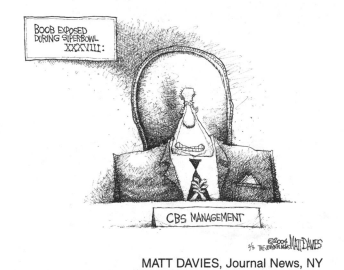

MATT DAVIES, Journal News, NY

REX BABIN, Sacramento Bee

BRUCE PLANTE, Chattanooga Times-Free Press

Howard Dean

Governor Howard Dean began his run for president with high hopes and a devout following.

He quickly became the front runner and unofficial Democratic nominee. All was going well, it seemed he could do no wrong ... and then came the "scream." At a raucous campaign rally, Dean yelled the names of states with upcoming primaries. People at the rally thought nothing of the scream, but on television and out of context, it seemed silly.

The media turned on Dean, replaying the scream over and over on TV. His campaign fizzled, leaving thousands of dedicated "Deaniacs" without their beloved new age, high-tech candidate.

www.CAGLECARTOONS.COM

SANDY HUFFAKER, Cagle Cartoons

15

DAN WASSERMAN, Boston Globe

MIKE LESTER, Rome News-Tribune, GA

JOHN COLE, Durham Herald-Sun

JOHN TREVER, Albuquerque Journal

CAL GRONDAHL, Utah Standard Examiner

Gay Marriage

Perhaps no other issue has proved as polarizing as gay marriage. This was the year that President Bush supported a constitutional amendment allowing states to ban gay marriage. A firestorm of criticism and media coverage followed as congress debated the issue.

Marriage licenses for gay couples were issued in California and Massachusetts. Some pundits say Bush rode the gay marriage election to his victory, as measures opposing gay marriage drove high voter turnout in key states.

When given the opportunity to tackle this issue, all of the cartoonists said "I do."

SAME-SEX WEDDING SEATING:

CHURCH STATE

USHER

MATT DAVIES,
Journal News, NY

MIKE LANE,
Baltimore Sun

SANDY HUFFAKER, Cagle Cartoons

JEFF PARKER, Florida Today

DICK WRIGHT, Tribune Media Services

STEVE SACK, Minneapolis Star-Tribune

DOUG MARLETTE, Tribune Media Services

20

AFTER MASSACHUSETTS GRANTS LEGALIZED SAME-SEX MARRIAGE, AMERICA FINDS ITSELF FOREVER AND INALTERABLY CHANGED...

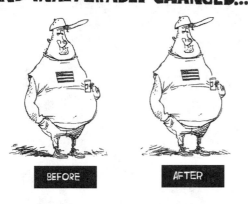

BEFORE

AFTER

MIKE LESTER, Rome News - Tribune, GA

ALL THIS TALK ABOUT SAME-SEX MARRIAGE IS CRAZY. NOTHING BEATS THE OLD STYLE OF MARRIAGE MY WIFE AND I HAVE ENJOYED FOR OVER 40 YEARS..

WE LIKE TO CALL IT A "NO-SEX" MARRIAGE.

CAMERON CARDOW,
Ottawa Citizen

STEVE SACK, Minneapolis Star-Tribune

WALT HANDELSMAN, Newsday

MIKE LESTER, Rome News-Tribune, GA

JOE HELLER, Green Bay Press-Gazetto

STEVE KELLEY, New Orleans Times-Picayune

DANA SUMMERS, Orlando Sentinel

GAY MARRIAGE

DARYL CAGLE, Slate.com

DICK LOCHER, Tribune Media Services

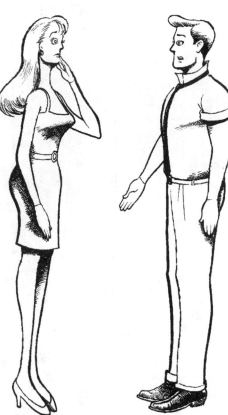

STEVE BREEN
San Diego Union-Tribune

MIKE LESTER
Rome News-Tribune, GA

THE HAPPY COUPLE WILL NOW CUT THE CAKE

MIKE LANE, Baltimore Sun

MY FELLOW HETEROS...

STATE OF A UNION IS BETWEEN A MAN AND A WOMAN.

GARY MARKSTEIN, Milwaukee Journal-Sentinel

MICHAEL RAMIREZ, Los Angeles Times

SHOTGUN WEDDING

25

DARYL CAGLE, Slate.com

 MIKE KEEFE,
Denver Post

GARY MARKSTEIN, Milwaukee Journal-Sentinel

JOE HELLER, Green Bay Press-Gazette

MARSHALL RAMSEY, Clarion Ledger

DREW SHENEMAN, Newark Star-Ledger

MIKE LESTER, Rome News - Tribune, GA

BOB GORRELL, AOL News

JOHN DEERING, Arkansas Democrat Gazette

DARYL CAGLE
Slate.com

WAYNE STAYSKAL, Tribune Media Services

Michael Moore

Filmmaker Michael Moore made the Most Likely Not To Get Invited To The White House Christmas Party list when he came out with his critically acclaimed and controversial film *Fahrenheit 911.*

Moore was previously known as the filmmaker behind *Roger & Me* and *Bowling For Columbine.* This time he went after the Bush administration, attempting to uncover the real reasons that the United States went to war with Iraq. The film and the issues that it raised divided the country and made an issue of Michael Moore himself.

OSMANI SIMANCA
Brazil

BRIAN FAIRRINGTON,
Cagle Cartoons

garbage in

garbage out

Facts?
What
Facts?

JEFF PARKER
Florida Today

OH LOOK, WARREN... NOW THAT THE FILM HAS ACTUALLY OPENED, YOU CAN FIND OUT IF THE OPINION YOU'VE ALREADY FORMED OF IT IS VALID OR NOT...

☆ NOW PLAYING ☆
FAHRENHEIT 9/11

caglecartoons.com

TAYLOR JONES
Tribune Media Services

31

JEFF STAHLER,
Cincinnati Post

MATT DAVIES, Journal News, NY

MICHAEL MOORE

JEFF STAHLER, Cincinnati Post

MIKE LANE,
Baltimore Sun

MIKE THOMPSON, Detroit Free-Press

"DID YOU KNOW THAT THE FLUORIDATION OF OUR WATER IS A BUSH PLOT TO POISON OUR BODILY FLUIDS?"

HENRY PAYNE, Detroit News

DREW SHENEMAN, Newark Star-Ledger

34

AND BUSH THOUGHT **SADDAM** HAD A WEAPON OF MASS DESTRUCTION!

MOORE

BOB GORRELL
AOL News

MIKE LESTER, Rome News-Tribune, GA

FAHRENHEIT 9/11

THE TIMES-PICAYUNE ©2004

I'M JOHN KERRY AND I APPROVED THIS MOVIE.

STEVE KELLEY, New Orleans Times-Picayune

MICHAEL RAMIREZ,
Los Angeles Times

MICHAEL MOORE OR LESS...

35

Martha Stewart

Martha Stewart cooked her own goose. After going on trial for lying to federal investigators about a deal involving her sale of IMClone stock, she was convicted and sentenced to six months in a federal prison.

Cartoonists pounce when the powerful fall. When asked by Barbara Walters what the worst thing was about going through this ordeal, Martha replied, "seeing those terribly mean cartoons."

Unfortunately for Martha, this was just an invitation for the cartoonists to turn up the heat.

TAYLOR JONES,
Tribune Media Services

www.reuben.org/jones/

MIKE KEEFE,
Denver Post

www.caglecartoons.com

"I can tell by the looks of your frumpy little outfit, and the sentence I got, that you never watched ANY of my shows!"

BRUCE BEATTIE,
Daytona News-Journal

CRUELLA DE-STEWART

DARYL CAGLE,
Slate.com

ERIC ALLIE, Pioneer Press, IL

GARY VARVEL, Indianapolis Star

JOE HELLER, Green Bay Press-Gazette

38

ROBERT ARIAIL,
The State, SC

R.J. MATSON, New York Observer

CLAY JONES
Fredericksburg Freelance-Star

DAVID FITZSIMMONS,
Arizona Daily Star

DARYL CAGLE,
Slate.com

CORPORATE FASHION UPDATE

ORANGE JUMPSUIT — MARTHA STEWART

ORANGE SWIMSUIT — KEN LAY / ENRON

GARY MARKSTEIN, Milwaukee Journal-Sentinel

HOW TO GET YOURSELF EXCLUDED FROM THE MARTHA STEWART JURY

I ESPECIALLY ENJOYED THE SHOW WHERE SHE BAKED THE CAKE WITH THE FILE IN IT...

BRUCE BEATTIE, Daytona News-Journal

JURY SELECTION FOR THE MARTHA STEWART TRIAL

NO, I'M SORRY... IT'S THE SALAD FORK ON THE OUTSIDE OF THE DINNER FORK... — NEXT!

MIKE LANE, Baltimore Sun

41

DWANE POWELL, Raleigh News & Observer

JOE HELLER
Green Bay
Press-Gazette

42

VINCE O'FARRELL
Illawarra Mercury

BRUCE PLANTE
Chattanooga Times Free-Press

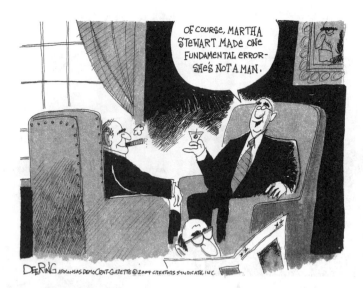

JOHN DEERING
Arkansas Democrat Gazette

STEVE BREEN
San Diego Union-Tribune

STEVE BENSON, Arizona Republic

44

JOHN DARKOW, Columbia Daily Tribune, MO

CLAY BENNETT, Christian Science Monitor

Michael Jackson

The media was obsessed with celebrity trials in 2004. Michael Jackson spent the year in and out of a Santa Maria, California courthouse, defending allegations of sexual misconduct with children who had been guests at his Neverland Ranch. Neverland is a large Disneyland-like compound that Jackson built outside of Santa Barbara, where he often invited children to parties with carnival rides and exotic animals. All of this gives new meaning to the term "petting zoo."

TAYLOR JONES
Tribune Media Services

©2004 Tribune Media Services, Inc.

46

MICHAEL RAMIREZ
Los Angeles Times

MIKE MIKULA
Rotundarama

CAM CARDOW, Ottawa Citizen

MIKE LESTER, Rome News-Tribune, GA

JIMMY MARGULIES, The Record, NJ

Parenting 101....

Don't let them play with loaded hand guns.

Don't let them play in the middle of the highway.

Don't let them sleep overnight in the same bed with a middle aged, surgically altered-pop star, has been, pedophile freak.

MICHAEL JACKSON

BRIAN FAIRRINGTON
Cagle Cartoons

JOHN DARKOW
Columbia Daily Tribune, MO

49

The Economy

The economy continued to go up and down like a roller coaster. 2004 may have been a good year to own stock in Tums or Pepto-Bismol. In a year when Americans were watching their 401K's shrink and their cost of living rise it seems we could all use some comic relief.

There was nothing funny about the economy in 2004, but that didn't stop the cartoonists.

THE CHRISTIAN SCIENCE MONITOR BENNETT

CLAY BENNETT, Christian Science Monitor

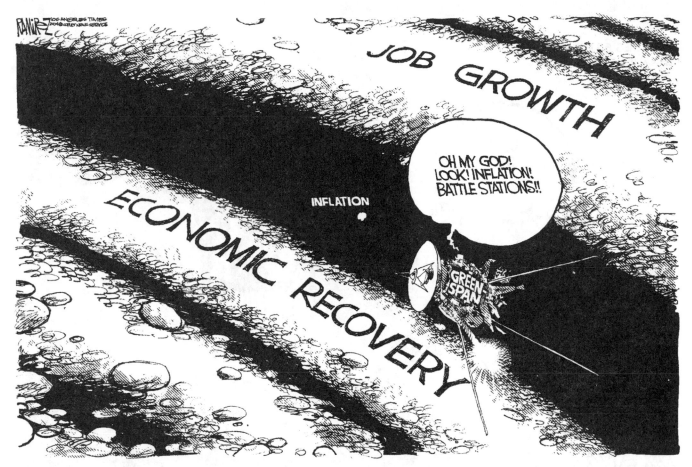

MICHAEL RAMIREZ, Los Angeles Times

BOB GORELL, AOL News

ROBERT ARIAIL, The State, SC

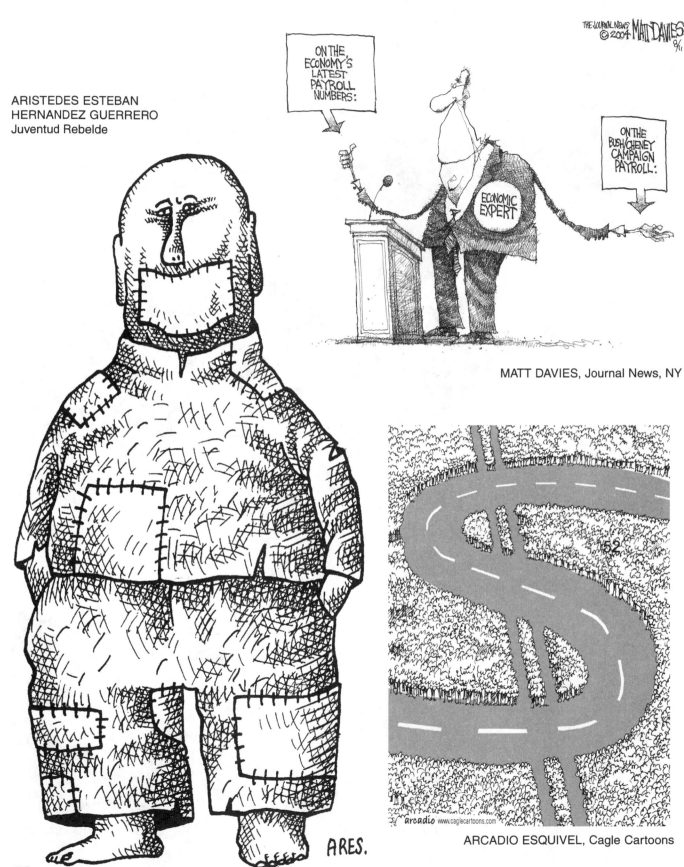

ARISTEDES ESTEBAN
HERNANDEZ GUERRERO
Juventud Rebelde

ARES.

MATT DAVIES, Journal News, NY

ARCADIO ESQUIVEL, Cagle Cartoons

ETTA HULME, Ft Worth Star Telegram

JEFF PARKER, Florida Today

ARCADIO ESQUIVEL, Cagle Cartoons

53

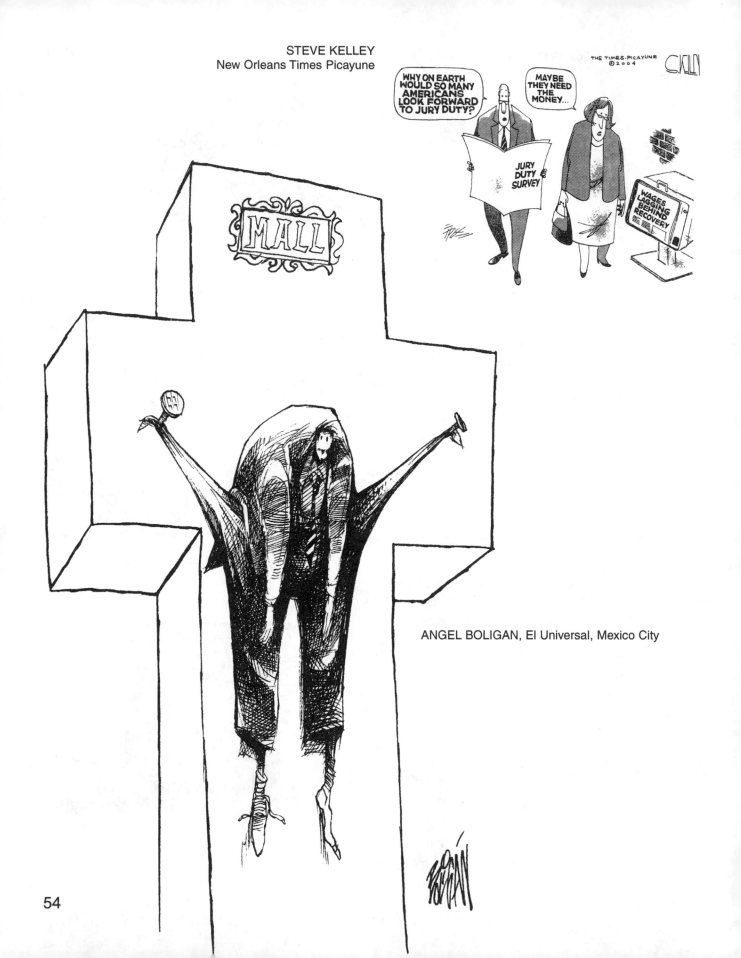

STEVE KELLEY
New Orleans Times Picayune

ANGEL BOLIGAN, El Universal, Mexico City

54

GARY VARVEL, Indianapolis Star

GARY MARKSTEIN, Milwaukee Journal-Sentinel

JEFF KOTERBA, Omaha World Herald

MARSHALL RAMSEY, Clarion Ledger

JOHN DEERING, Arkansas Democrat Gazette

JOHN TREVER, Albuquerque Journal

REX BABIN, Sacramento Bee

ETTA HULME, Ft. Worth Star-Telegram

BRUCE PLANTE, Chattanooga Times Free Press

JOE HELLER, Green Bay Press-Gazette

CLAY BENNETT
Christian Science Montior

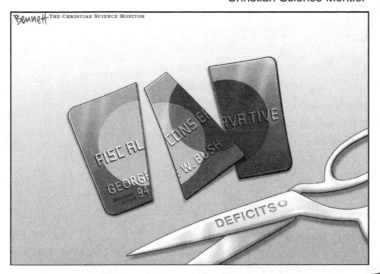

JAMES CASCIARI,
Scripps Howard

Healthcare

Healthcare was a hot issue as we all tried to manage the steep costs of health insurance and prescription drugs. Politicians continued to debate the methods of curing our healthcare ills, Medicare drug discounts, and cheaper imported drugs from Canada. Cartoonists coughed up enough cartoons about healthcare in 2004 to make anyone sick.

STEVE SACK, Minneapolis Star-Tribune

STEVE BREEN, San Diego Union-Tribune

MIKE KEEFE, Denver Post

DANA SUMMERS
Orlando Sentinel

BOB ENGLEHART, Hartford Courant

60

JIMMY MARGULIES, The Record, NJ

JOE HELLER, Green Bay Press Gazette

DAVID HORSEY, Seattle Post-Intelligencer

Prescriptions

JIMMY MARGULIES, The Record, NJ

JEFF STAHLER, Cincinnati Post

MIKE LANE, Baltimore Sun

GARY MARKSTEIN, Milwaukee Journal-Sentinel

SUMMER READING

STEVE BREEN, San Diego Union-Tribune

GARY VARVEL, Indianapolis Star

SANDY HUFFAKER, Cagle Cartoons

JOHN DEERING, Arkansas Democrat Gazette

JOHN DARKOW, Columbia Daily Tribune, MO

63

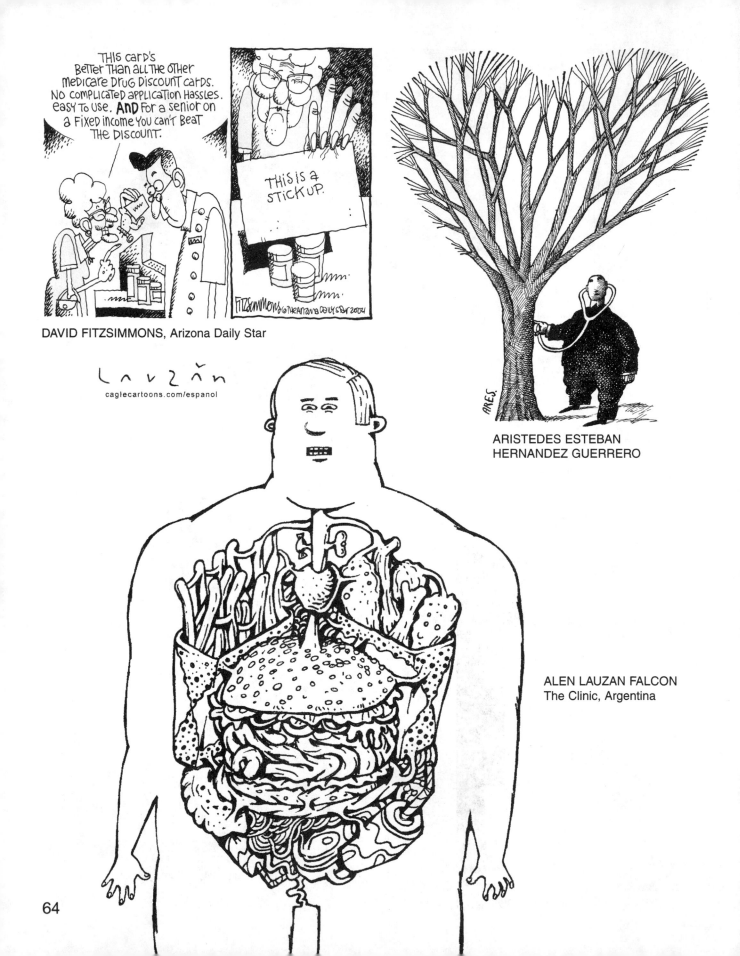

DAVID FITZSIMMONS, Arizona Daily Star

ARISTEDES ESTEBAN
HERNANDEZ GUERRERO

ALEN LAUZAN FALCON
The Clinic, Argentina

64

JEFF PARKER
Florida Today

REX BABIN, Sacramento Bee

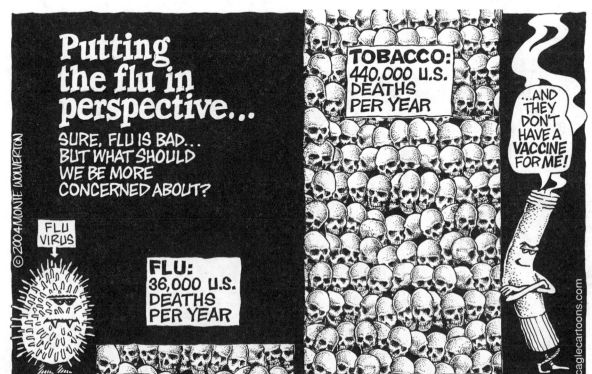

MONTE
WOLVERTON
Cagle
Cartoons

65

BRUCE PLANTE, Chattanooga Times Free-Press

MIKE THOMPSON, Detroit Free-Press

ED STEIN, Rocky Mountain News

ED STEIN, Rocky Mountain News

HENRY PAYNE, Detroit News

Environment

Global warming, world population, shrinking rain forests, and dependency on fossil fuels continue to be controversial issues in the news. In an overly crowded world, it comes as no surprise that we're over-crowded with cartoons on the environment. In 2004, newspapers from around the world cut down many acres of trees to make the paper on which they printed environmentally conscious cartoons, like these ...

JEFF PARKER, Florida Today

BRUCE BEATTIE, Daytona News-Journal

HENRY PAYNE, Detroit News

ARISTEDES ESTEBAN
HERNANDEZ GUERRERO
Juventud Rebelde

ᒐ ᐱ ᐁ ᕗ ᐩ

ALEN LAUZAN FALCON, The Clinic

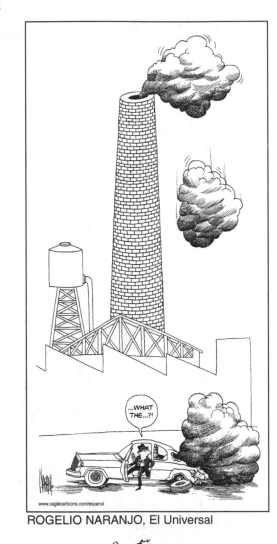

...WHAT THE...?!

www.caglecartoons.com/espanol

ROGELIO NARANJO, El Universal

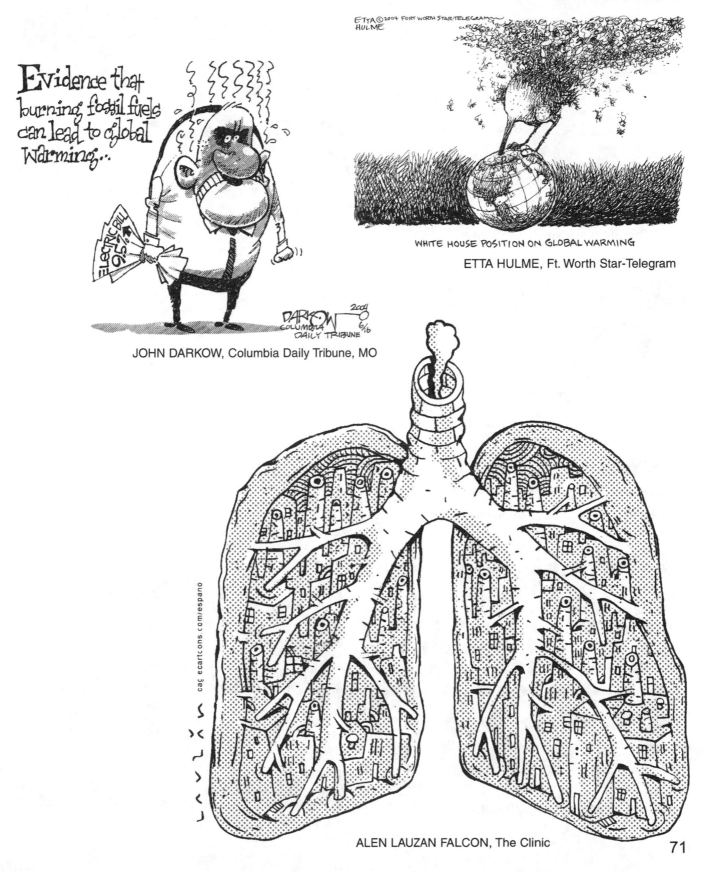

Evidence that burning fossil fuels can lead to global warming...

JOHN DARKOW, Columbia Daily Tribune, MO

WHITE HOUSE POSITION ON GLOBAL WARMING

ETTA HULME, Ft. Worth Star-Telegram

ALEN LAUZAN FALCON, The Clinic

71

STEVE BREEN, San Diego Union-Tribune

BRUCE PLANTE, Chattanooga Times Free Press

MONTE WOLVERTON, Cagle Cartoons

WAYNE STAYSKAL, Tribune Media Services

STEVE GREENBERG, Ventura Star, CA

MIKE THOMPSON, Detroit Free-Press

REMEMBER WHEN WE DID THAT WITH SHELLS ?...

ROBERT ARIAIL, The State, SC

ALEN LAUZAN FALCON, The Clinic

JIM MORIN, Miami Herald

Year of the Storms

In an election year, the hot air usually blows in from the candidates; this year was an exception as we saw Mother Nature shower the East Coast with an unprecedented storm season. Florida was at the center of the brutal assault that began with Hurricane Charley and continued with Frances, which hit the Florida Peninsula, and Ivan, which pounded the Panhandle, paving destruction all the way up to the Alabama coast. Many of the nation's top cartoonists reside in Florida and other hurricane ravaged areas, providing a poignant look at life from inside the eye of the storm.

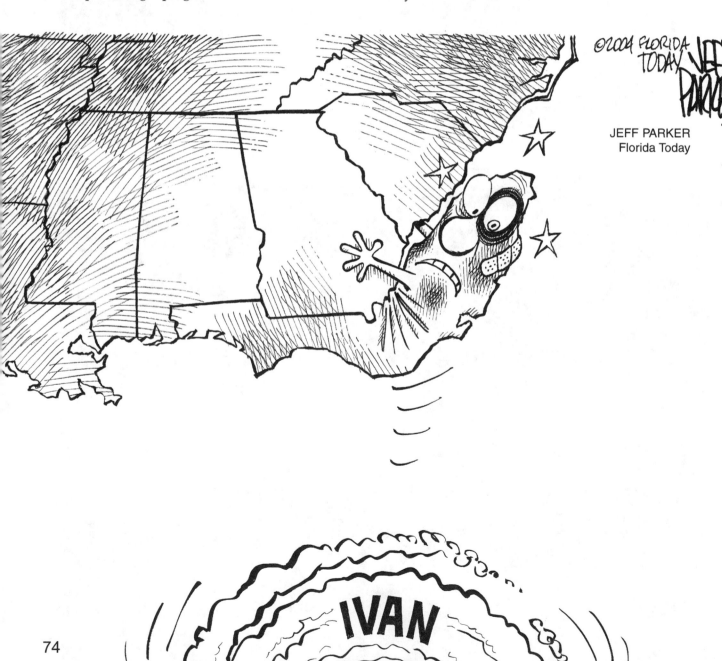

©2004 FLORIDA TODAY JEFF PARKER

jparker@flatoday.net

JEFF PARKER
Florida Today

IVAN

ROBERT ARIAIL, The State, SC

JIM MORIN, Miami Herald

PUNCHING BAG

75

WALT HANDELSMAN, Newsday

MARSHALL RAMSEY, Clarion Ledger

BOB GORELL, AOL News

J.D. CROWE
Mobile Register

MIKE LESTER, Rome News-Tribune (GA)

DANA SUMMERS,
Orlando Sentinel

PAUL COMBS

MIKE KEEFE,
Denver Post

MARK STREETER, Savannah Morning News

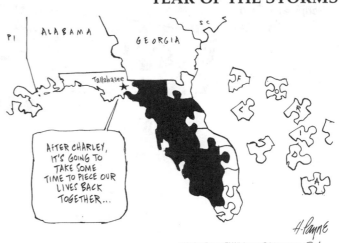

HENRY PAYNE, Detroit News

CHUCK ASAY, Colorado Springs Gazette

STEVE KELLEY, New Orleans Times Picayune

BRUCE BEATTIE, Daytona News-Journal

JIM DAY, Las Vegas Review-Journal

JAMES CASCIARI
Scripps Howard
News Service

CHIP BOK, Akron Beacon-Journal

MIKE THOMPSON, Detroit Free-Press

JIM MORIN, Miami Herald

War in Iraq

The war became the central issue during 2004 as those who supported military action in the beginning began to express doubts about the conflict and the lack of an apparent exit strategy. The Bush administration continued to defend its decision to invade Iraq, despite growing concerns over the costs and casualties of the war.

R.J. MATSON, Roll Call

MILT PRIGGEE

...THEY'LL BE GREETED WITH FLOWERS...

WALT HANDELSMAN, Newsday

IRAQ WAR MEMORIAL-PROPOSAL

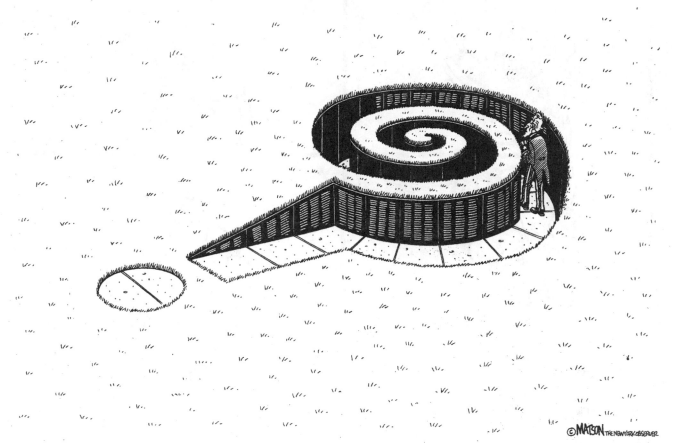

R.J. MATSON, New York Observer

DANA SUMMERS, Orlando Sentinel

DAVID CATROW, Springfield News-Sun, OH

THE HAND-OVER

85

DENNIS DRAUGHON, Scranton Times

CLAY BENNETT
Christian Science Monitor

CHRIS BRITT,
State Journal-Register, IL

DICK LOCHER, Chicago Tribune

CORKY TRINIDAD,
Honolulu Star Bulletin

TURNOVER

STEVE SACK, Minneapolis Star-Tribune

BILL DAY,
Memphis Commercial-Appeal

CAL GRONDAHL
Standard Examiner, Utah

"Exit strategy? That's a good question."

CHILDREN OF SADDAM...

DAVID HORSEY
Seattle Post Intelligencer

JOHN SHERFFIUS

PATRICK CHAPPATTE
International Herald Tribune

STEVE GREENBERG, Ventura Star, CA

PANDORA'S BOTTLE

"WE STILL HAVE NO DOUBT GOING INTO IRAQ MADE AMERICA SAFER..."

"...BUT NOT THE MIDDLE EAST."

CORKY TRINIDAD, Honolulu Star-Bulletin

PAUL COMBS, Tampa Tribune

DARYL CAGLE, Slate.com

91

KIRK ANDERSON

PATRICK O'CONNOR, Los Angeles Daily News

BILL SCHORR, AM New York

CLAY BENNETT
Christian Science Monitor

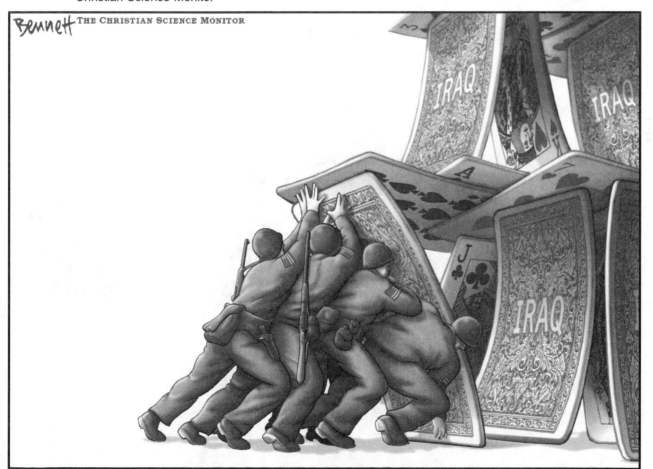

'WE'RE READY TO BEGIN PRE-BOARDING...'

STEVE SACK, Minneapolis Star-Tribune

PATRICK CHAPPATTE
International Herald Tribune

PAUL CONRAD,
Tribune Media
Services

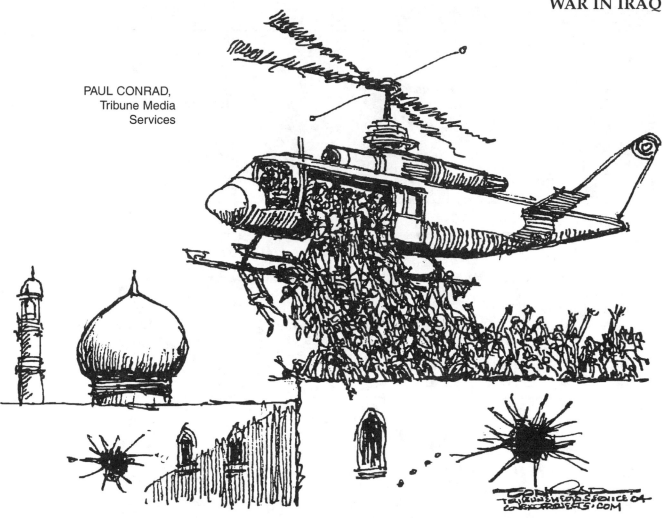

EXIT STRATEGY: DECLARE VICTORY AND PULL OUT.

WALT HANDELSMAN, Newsday

IF a TREE FaLLS IN THE FOREST aND NO ONE IS aROUND TO HEaR IT, DOES IT MaKE a SOUND?...

IF a SOLDIER FaLLS IN BaTTLE aND NO ONE IS aLLOWED TO SEE IT...

CENSORED

DENNIS DRAUGHON, Scranton Times

U.N.

...THE PRESIDENT GIVES AN UPBEAT ASSESSMENT OF THE WAR IN IRAQ...

BUT FIRST— A LOOK AT TODAY'S BEHEADING...

95

TROUBLETOWN

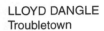
LLOYD DANGLE
Troubletown

Panel 1: AS IF THE SOLDIERS DIDN'T HAVE ENOUGH PROBLEMS...

I COULDN'T AVOID TELLING YOU ANY LONGER, MR. RUMSFELD. WE'RE OUT OF BULLETS.

OH, CRAP!

Panel 2: BUT OUR TROOPS' SUPERIOR TRAINING PREPARES THEM TO DEAL WITH ANY SITUATION.

THE OLD SOFT SHOE?

SKIP TIPPETY TAP!

TAP! TAPPITY TAP!

Panel 3: THE NATIONAL GUARD UNITS ARE NOT SO LUCKY.

FIRST WE HAD TO BRING OUR OWN BODY ARMOR AND HUMVEES. NOW WE ARE ASKED TO BRING OUR OWN AMMO!

I FEEL JUST LIKE A SCHOOL TEACHER.

Panel 4: THE COMPANY CONTRACTED TO SUPPLY BULLETS FOR IRAQ, ARMRON, IS COINCIDENTALLY CLOSELY TIED TO THE BUSH AND CHENEY FAMILIES!

WHAT CAN I DO? THERE'S A **SHORTAGE!** DEMAND IS UP! WE MUST RAISE PRICES TO $5 A BULLET!

HEE HEE!

Panel 5: THIS AFFECTS THE DOMESTIC BULLET MARKET AND AMERICANS ARE ASKED TO SACRIFICE!

SORRY, BULLET RATIONING. TWO PER PERSON.

B-BUT MY WIFE IS SEEING ANOTHER GUY!

NO!

Panel 6: AND SO, IRONICALLY, THE DISASTER IN IRAQ BRINGS PEACE & HARMONY TO THE STREETS OF AMERICA!

I'D BUST A CAP IN YO ASS BUT I'M OUT OF BULLETS!

ANDRE.

ME TOO. SO WHAT'S YOUR NAME?

I'M RICHIE.

© 2004

WWW.TROUBLETOWN.COM

PAUL CONRAD
Tribune Media
Services

96

MATT DAVIES, Journal News, NY

TIM MENEES, Pittsburgh Post-Gazette

GARY VARVEL, Indianapolis Star

Saddam Hussein

Saddam Hussein was found by U.S. soldiers just outside Baghdad hiding in a "spider hole" that was barely larger than a coffin. Today Saddam sits in a somewhat larger cell in an undisclosed prison location waiting to go on trial for his many heinous crimes. Over the past fifteen years, Saddam Hussein has been a favorite character for the world's editorial cartoonists. The new Iraqi government will probably try to execute Saddam, leaving the world without one of our favorite cartoon characters.

The cartoonists will grieve.

Well, maybe not.

TAYLOR JONES
Tribune Media Services

DICK WRIGHT, Tribune Media Services

LARRY WRIGHT, Detroit News

JAMES CASCIARI
Scripps Howard News Service

CRIMES AGAINST HUMANITY

MICHAEL RAMIREZ
Los Angeles Times

THE CASE AGAINST SADDAM

JIMMY MARGULIES, The Record, NJ

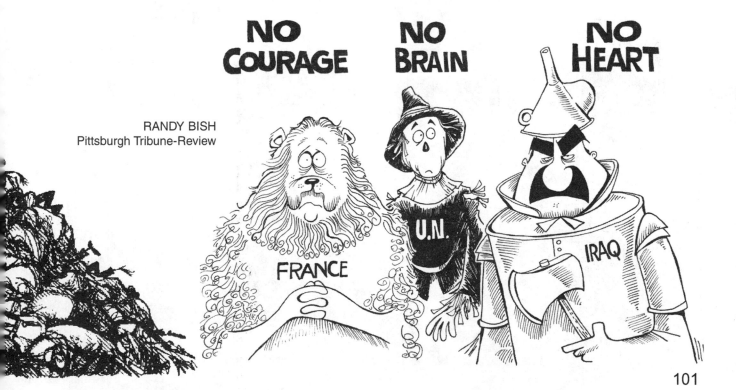

RANDY BISH
Pittsburgh Tribune-Review

ROBERT ARIAIL
The State, SC

JIM MORIN, Miami Herald

SADDAM HUSSEIN

CHIP BOK, Akron Beacon-Journal

GARY VARVEL, Indianapolis Star

VINCE O'FARRELL, Illawarra Mercury, Australia

103

JOHN DARKOW, Columbia Daily Tribune, MO

CHRIS BRITT, State Journal-Register, IL

BRUCE PLANTE
Chattanooga Times Free Press

STEVE KELLEY, New Orleans Times Picayune

JOHN TREVER
Albuquerque Journal

Where's Osama?

Osama Bin Laden, the mastermind behind the 2001 World Trade Center attacks, remains on the loose despite America's best efforts to capture him. The Bush Administration declared war on terrorism and those that harbor terrorists, including Saddam Hussein. While Saddam was captured, Bin Laden escaped somewhere in the mountains of Afghanistan. He is reported to have severe kidney problems.

All of this begs the question: why can't the U.S. find a six-foot-five Arab dragging a dialysis machine through the desert?

ARISTEDES ESTEBAN
HERNANDEZ GUERRERO
Juventud Rebelde

ARES.

CAMERON CARDOW
Ottawa Citizen

DAVID HORSEY, Seattle Post Intelligence

LARRY WRIGHT, Detroit News

CHRIS BRITT, State Journal-Register, IL

ROBERT ARIAIL
The State, SC

JOHN DARKOW, Columbia Daily Tribune, MO

KIRK ANDERSON

BOB ENGLEHART, Hartford Courant

110

SIMANCA OSMANI
Brazil

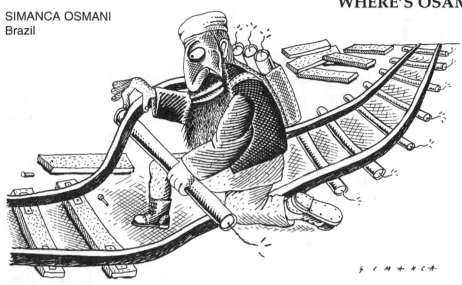

DARYL CAGLE, Slate.com

111

Oil

America's dependency on fossil fuels continues to be an issue of great debate among those who continue to rely on oil and those who believe in alternative sources of fuel. Cartoonists throughout the country jumped on this issue by jumping in their SUVs and using lots of gas in order to get down to their art supply store to buy lots of ink to draw more cartoons about people using lots of oil. Cartoonists love irony.

BILL SCHORR,
AM New York

The Junkie

MIKE KEEFE,
Denver Post

DICK LOCHER, Tribune Media Services

MIKE KEEFE, Denver Post

BRUCE BEATTIE
Daytona News-Journal

114

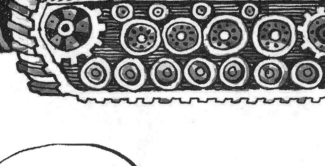

SIMANCA OSMANI
Brazil

The Clarion-Ledger
COPLEY NEWS SERVICE

THANK GOD ITS DROPPING...

ECONOMY

OIL PRICES

MARSHALL RAMSEY
Clarion Ledger

STEVE BREEN
San Diego Union-Tribune

SERGIO LANGER, El Clarin, Argentina

OIL

ROBERT ARIAIL
The State, SC

BOB GORRELL, AOL News

117

PATRICK CHAPPATTE, International Herald Tribune

M.e. COHEN

GRAEME MACKAY, Hamilton Spectator

ARISTEDES ESTEBAN
HERNANDEZ GUERRERO
Juventud Rebelde

ARES.
caglecartoons.com/espanol

STEVE GREENBERG, Ventura Star, CA

WAYNE
STAYSKAL
Tampa Tribune

120

OIL

JIM DAY
Las Vegas Review-Journal

121

ARISTEDES ESTEBAN
HERNANDEZ GUERRERO
Juventud Rebelde

PAUL CONRAD
Tribune Media Services

BRIAN FAIRRINGTON
Cagle Cartoons

WHERE THE DINOSAURS GO TO DIE ?

MIKE LANE, Baltimore Sun

LARRY WRIGHT, Detroit News

MIKE LESTER, Rome News-Tribune

DANA SUMMERS, Orlando Sentinel

The Olympics

Once again the Olympics were tainted with allegations of drug abuse. This year, however, the games in Athens had to deal with the additional on-going threat of terrorism. The games began with unusually tight security with check points and lines to get into the events that were longer than ever. The Greeks finished building the Olympic venues at the last minute. Small crowds were a problem as television audiences were surprised to see empty seats as a backdrop to the events. America was shocked by the poor performance of their all-star, basketball "dream team." Despite the problems, the games were declared a success and, for a brief moment, the world seemed to get along.

KEVIN KALLAUGHER, Baltimore Sun, CWS/CartoonArts International

FIND THE SPECTATOR...

STEVE BREEN, San Diego Union-Tribune

DANA SUMMERS
Orlando Sentinel

125

STEVE KELLEY, New Orleans Times Picayune

ROBERT ARIAIL, The State, SC

JEFF KOTERBA, Omaha World Herald

JOE HELLER, Green Bay Press-Gazette

MARSHALL RAMSEY, Clarion Ledger

GARY MARKSTEIN, Milwaukee Journal-Sentinel

VIC HARVILLE, Stephens Media Group

caglecartoons.com/espanol
ANGEL BOLIGAN, El Universal, Mexico

STEVE GREENBERG, Ventura Star, CA

POST-ATHENS EVENT
JEFF KOTERBA, Omaha World Herald

BOB ENGLEHART, Hartford Courant

127

MIKE KEEFE, Denver Post

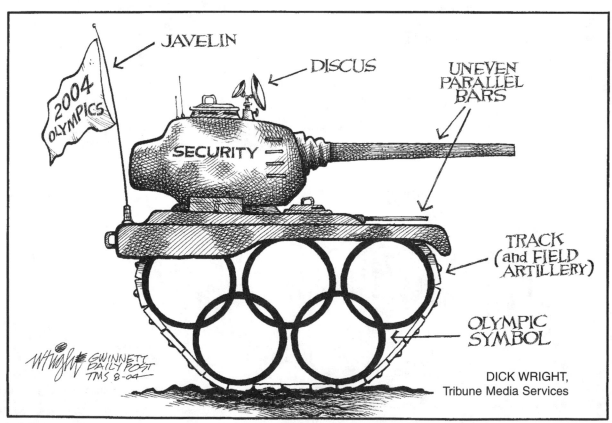

DICK WRIGHT,
Tribune Media Services

128

BOB GORRELL, AOL News

BOB ENGLEHART, Hartford Courant

DICK LOCHER, Chicago Tribune

ARCADIO ESQUIVEL, La Prensa, Panama

HENRY PAYNE, Detroit News

VINCE O'FARRELL, Cagle Cartoons

THE OLYMPICS

129

BILL DAY, Memphis Commercial-Appeal

CAL GRONDAHL
Utah Standard Examiner

GARY VARVEL, Indianapolis Star

MIKE THOMPSON, Detroit Free-Press

STEVE BREEN, San Diego Union-Tribune

BRUCE PLANTE, Chattanooga Times Free Press

BOB GORRELL, AOL News

J.D. CROWE, Mobile Register

131

BRUCE BEATTIE, Daytona News-Journal

Attendance Sparse at Athens Olympics

JEFF DANZIGER, CWS/CartoonArts International

BILL SCHORR
AM New York

JEFF STAHLER, Columbus Dispatch

RANDY BISH, Pittsburgh Tribune-Review

JIMMY MARGULIES, The Record

ROB ROGERS, Pittsburgh Post-Gazette

134

ROBERT ARIAIL
The State, SC

CAMERON CARDOW
Ottawa Citizen

135

Terrorism

Terrorism continues to be a central concern in the lives of Americans. From the constant, ugly stream of news coming from the Middle East to color coded terror alerts. We learned that North Korea had a number of nuclear bombs, and Iran was soon to develop the bomb. The CIA and FBI seemed incompetent. The world was a scary place.

DARYL CAGLE, Slate.com

MIKE KEEFE
Denver Post

CLAY BENNETT
Christian Science
Monitor

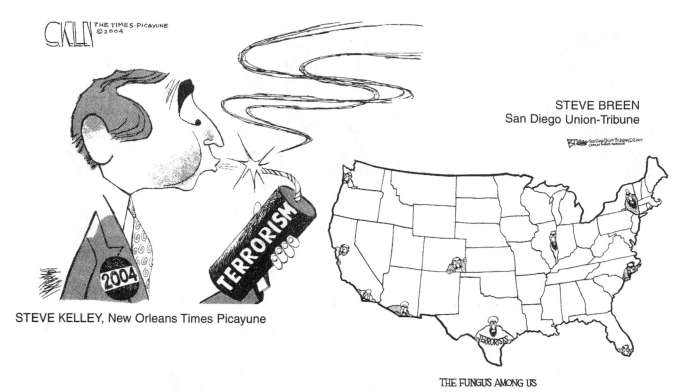

STEVE KELLEY, New Orleans Times Picayune

STEVE BREEN
San Diego Union-Tribune

THE FUNGUS AMONG US

CLAY BENNETT, Christian Science Monitor

"AROUND AND AROUND IT GOES. WHERE IT LANDS, NOBODY KNOWS..."

GARY MARKSTEIN, Milwaukee Journal-Sentinel

"IT'S FORECAST TO TOUCH DOWN SOMETIME, SOMEPLACE THIS SUMMER!"

BOB ENGLEHART, Hartford Courant

WAYNE STAYSKAL, Tribune Media Services

SLOWPOKE

JEN SORENSON
Slowpoke

Panel 1: THE DEPARTMENT OF HOMELAND SECURITY MAKES A SPECIAL ANNOUNCEMENT.

OUR CAMPAIGN— I MEAN, OUR COUNTRY— FACES A GRAVE AND CONSTANT THREAT. DOOM COULD COME AT ANY MOMENT.

BUT THERE'S SOMETHING YOU CAN DO: BEGIN WEARING A **TERROR-FIGHTING HAT.**

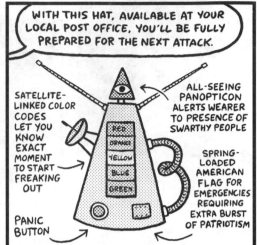

Panel 2: WITH THIS HAT, AVAILABLE AT YOUR LOCAL POST OFFICE, YOU'LL BE FULLY PREPARED FOR THE NEXT ATTACK.

SATELLITE-LINKED COLOR CODES LET YOU KNOW EXACT MOMENT TO START FREAKING OUT

ALL-SEEING PANOPTICON ALERTS WEARER TO PRESENCE OF SWARTHY PEOPLE

SPRING-LOADED AMERICAN FLAG FOR EMERGENCIES REQUIRING EXTRA BURST OF PATRIOTISM

PANIC BUTTON

RED
ORANGE
YELLOW
BLUE
GREEN

Panel 3: MILLIONS OF AMERICANS DUTIFULLY DON THE HATS.

HE WILL KEEP US SAFE
W - 2004

HEY, THAT GUY DOESN'T HAVE A HAT!

I'M HITTING MY PANIC BUTTON!

Panel 4: SOON, ANOTHER TERROR-FIGHTING TOOL IS OFFERED.

THIS AMULET CONTAINING A HAIR FROM THE PRESIDENT, POWDERED RAM'S HORN, AND RATTLESNAKE FANG WILL CONFER OUR LEADER'S MANLY STRENGTH UPON YOU.

YOURS FOR ONLY A $100 DONATION TO THE REPUBLICAN NATIONAL COMMITTEE!

www.slowpokecomics.com

The Nightmare of Sam Gulliver

ALEN LAUZAN FALCON, The Clinic, Chile

JIMMY MARGULIES, The Record, NJ

WAYNE STAYSKAL, Tribune Media Services

STEVE KELLEY, New Orleans Times Picayune

SUMMER TERROR WARNING...

ELECTION UNDECIDEDS

ETTA HULME
Ft. Worth Star-Telegram

ETTA © 2004 FORT WORTH STAR·TELEGRAM
HULME

CLUE

ARCADIO ESQUIVEL
La Prensa, Panama

arcadio/CAGLECARTOONS.COM

U.S. INTELLIGENCE

SIMANCA
OSMANI
Brazil

SIMANCA

143

MICHAEL RAMIREZ, Los Angeles Times

STEVE SACK
Minneapolis
Star-Tribune

CHRIS BRITT, State Journal-Register, IL

BRUCE BEATTIE, Daytona News-Journal

OLLE JOHANSSON
Nora Vasterbotten
Sweden

BILL DAY, Memphis Commercial-Appeal

MIKE LESTER
Rome News
Tribune, GA

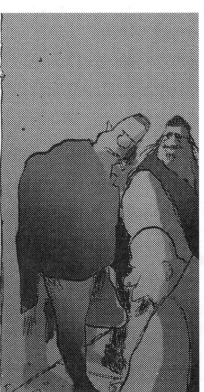

CHIP BOK
Akron Beacon Journal

Abu Ghraib Prison

In an ongoing effort to win the hearts and minds of the Iraqi people, the Abu Ghraib Prison scandal couldn't have come at a worse time. Photos surfaced showing the abuse of Iraqi prisoners by U.S. soldiers and fueled an already heated debate over America's involvement in Iraq. The photos were seen across the world where many viewed them only as recruiting posters for terrorism.

STEVE BREEN,
San Diego
Union-Tribune

MIKE THOMPSON, Detroit Free-Press

JACK OHMAN
Portland
Oregonian

149

BOB ENGLEHART, Hartford Courant

DARYL CAGLE, Slate.com

JIMMY MARGULIES, The Record, NJ

MIKE KEEFE, Denver Post

MICHAEL RAMIREZ, Los Angeles Times

KEPT IN THE DARK

CAL GRONDAHL, Utah Standard Examiner

The MORAL Compass

DAVID CATROW, Springfield News-Sun

PAUL CONRAD
Tribune Media Services

THE COVER-UP

STEVE GREENBERG, Ventura Star, CA

WHAT HAPPENED TO THE VALUES WE PROJECT TO THE WORLD?

DENNIS DRAUGHON, Scranton Times

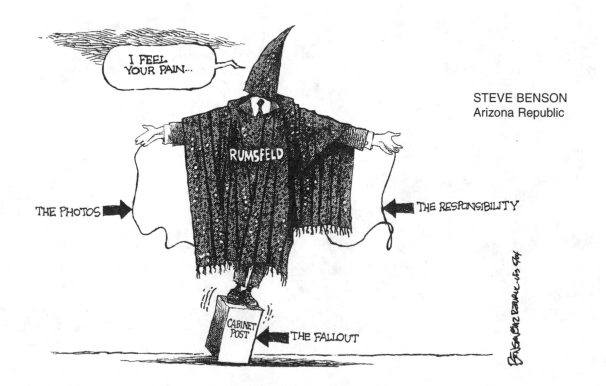

STEVE BENSON
Arizona Republic

152

BOB GORRELL, AOL News

GARY MARKSTEIN, Milwaukee Journal-Sentinel

ROBERT ARIAIL, The State, SC

PATRICK O'CONNOR, Los Angeles Daily News

153

CHRIS BRITT, State Journal-Register

MARSHALL RAMSEY, Clarion Ledger

JEFF KOTERBA, Omaha World Herald

BOLIGAN
El Universal, Mexico

JOHN TREVER, Albuquerque Journal

BILL DAY, Memphis Commercial-Appeal

ROB ROGERS, Pittsburg Post-Gazette

BRUCE BEATTIE, Daytona News-Journal

JIM MORIN
Miami Herald

DREW SHENEMAN, Newark Star-Ledger

"SECRETARY RUMSFELD, DO YOU HAVE TIME FOR A QUICK PHOTO?"

ETTA HULME, Ft. Worth Star Telegram

157

JOHN COLE, Durham Herald-Sun

PATRICK CHAPPATTE
International
Herald Tribune

158

JOHN DARKOW, Columbia Daily Tribune, MO

ABU GHRAIB PRISON

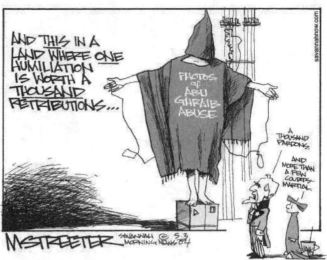

MARK STREETER, Savannah Morning News

JOHN SHERFFIUS
© 5-11-04 jsherffius@aol.com

Rumsfailed

159

DARYL CAGLE, Slate.com

MARK STREETER, Savannah Morning News

TIM MENEES, Pittsburgh Post-Gazette

9/11 Commission

After September 11th, many in Washington called for an investigation into the causes and subsequent failures of the government to detect the attacks. On the heels of 9/11, the Bush administration used questionable intelligence to justify going to war with Iraq, citing a connection between Saddam Hussein and Osama Bin Laden. The 9/11 Commission convened on Capital Hill and heard testimony from hundreds of officials from all aspects of U.S. Intelligence. Most, if not all, of those who testified indicated that there was no direct connection between Bin Laden and Hussein. In light of this new information, the commission published the 9/11 report, stating their findings.

STEVE SACK, Minneapolis Star-Tribune

THE 9-11 HEARINGS...

DICK WRIGHT,
Tribune Media Services

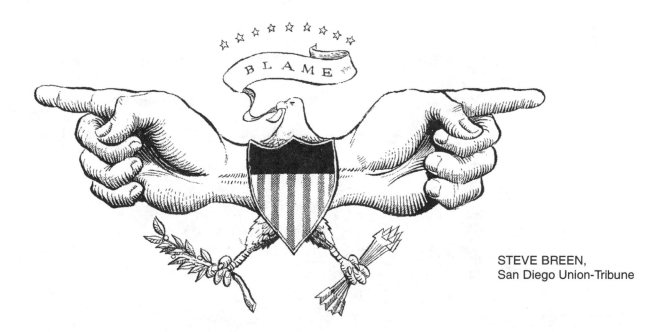

STEVE BREEN,
San Diego Union-Tribune

163

JACK OHMAN, Portland Oregonian

SANDY
HUFFAKER,
Cagle Cartoons

GARY VARVEL, Indianapolis Star

MATT WUERKER, Lint Trap

DENNIS DRAUGHON, Scranton Times

CORKY TRINIDAD, Honolulu Star Bulletin

MARK STREETER, Savannah Morning News

REX BABIN
Sacramento Bee

STEVE SACK
Minneapolis
Star-Tribune

MAYBE IT WAS A MISTAKE TO LET THEM TESTIFY TOGETHER....

ED STEIN, Rocky Mountain News

MARK STREETER, Savannah Morning News

JIMMY MARGULIES, The Record

GARY MARKSTEIN, Milwaukee Journal-Sentinel

M.e. COHEN

BOB ENGLEHART, Hartford Courant

LARRY WRIGHT, Detroit News

BRUCE PLANTE, Chattannoga Times Free Press

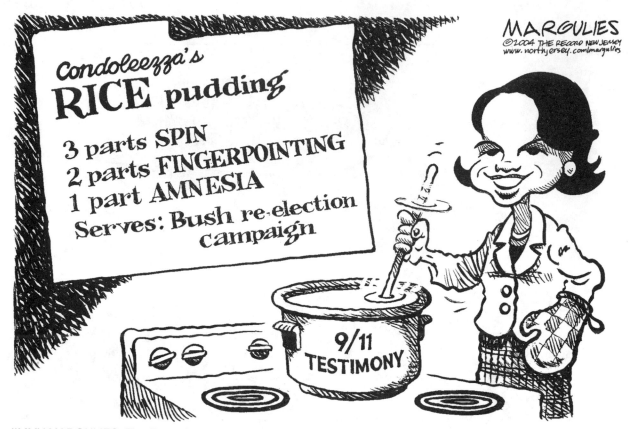

JIMMY MARGULIES, The Record

JEFF PARKER
Florida Today

DARYL CAGLE
Slate.com

National Security Advisor Condoleezza Rice
refuses to testify in public for the 9/11 Commission.

M. e. COHEN

Russian School Terror

The world was shocked and saddened when Muslim terrorists engaged in a week long stand off at an elementary school in Russia on the opening day of the new fall semester.

The terrorists held the children and teachers hostage while anxious parents held a round-the-clock vigil just outside. Sadly, when the smoke cleared an estimated two hundred people were killed, mostly children.

This grim incident added to the growing list of terrorist attacks that were becoming more commonplace in 2004.

ANGEL BOLIGAN
El Universal
Mexico

THE SEPARATIST...

VINCE O'FARRELL
The Illawarra Mercury
Australia

www.caglecartoons.com

JIM MORIN, Miami Herald

FACE-TO-FACE...

173

JIMMY MARGULIES, The Record, NJ

DARYL CAGLE
Slate.com

JOHN COLE, Durham Herald-Sun

PAUL COMBS

ROBERT ARIAIL, The State, SC

Bush Bashing

George W. Bush has been commander in chief during one of the most difficult times in American history. Immediately following 9/11 his approval ratings were at an all time high for any U.S. president and his deadfast resolve united the country. However, Bush's decision to go to war with Iraq had a polarizing effect on the country and set the stage for one of the most heated elections in modern American history. In 2004, cartoonists drew more "Bush bashing" cartoons than anything else. Bush, the cartoon character, evolved into a bizarre charater with giant ears and eyebrows, a huge upper lip and beady little eyes.

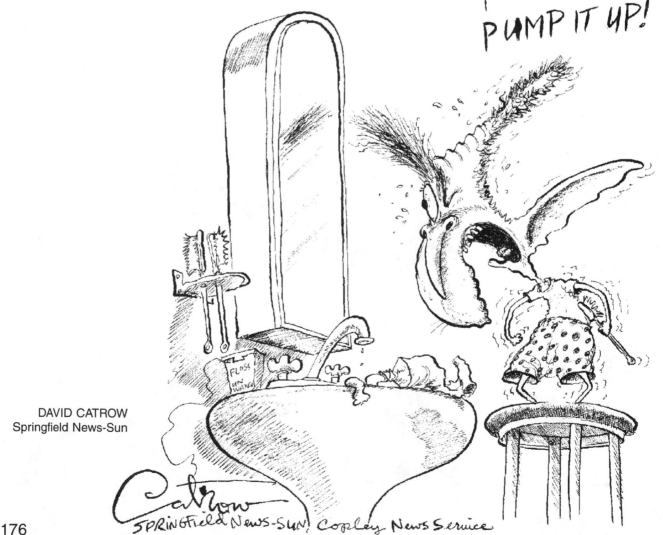

YOU DA MAN! YOU BAD! YOU DA PREZ GOT the MORAL HIGH GROUND, GOT IT GOOD, GOOOOOD! PUMP IT, PUMP IT UP!

DAVID CATROW
Springfield News-Sun

STEVE SACK
Minneapolis Star-Tribune

THe WiND BeNeATH MY WiNGS....

MARK STREETER, Savannah Morning News

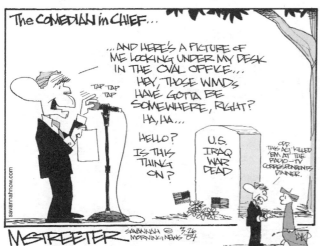

DAN WASSERMAN, Boston Globe

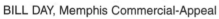

BILL DAY, Memphis Commercial-Appeal

178

THE "STRAIGHT SHOOTER"

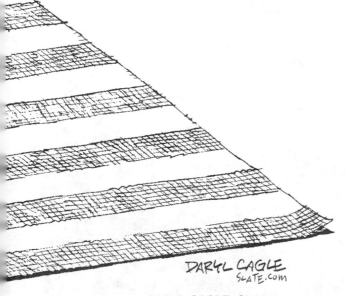

DARYL CAGLE, Slate.com

JIMMY MARGULIES, The Record, NJ

179

AWOL

CHRIS BRITT, State Journal-Sentinel, IL

STEVE BREEN
San Diego Union-Tribune

CHRIS BRITT, State Journal-Sentinel, IL

R.J. MATSON, Roll Call

MICHAEL DEADDER, Halifax Daily News

MIKE KEEFE, Denver Post

JOHN DEERING, Arkansas Democrat Gazette

DAVID HORSEY, Seattle Post Intelligencer

JEFF STAHLER
Columbus Dispatch

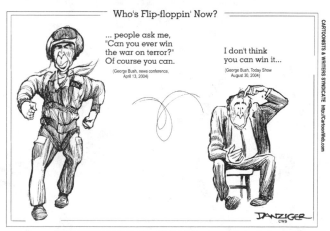

JEFF DANZIGER, CWS/CartoonArts International

KIRK ANDERSON

ROBERT ARIAIL, The State, SC

KEVIN KALLAUGHER, Baltimore Sun
CWS/CartoonArts International

STEVE SACK
Minneapolis Star-Tribune

STEVE BENSON, Arizona Republic

PATRICK CHAPPATTE
International Herald Tribune

JOHN COLE, Durham Herald-Sun

187

DAVID CATROW, Springfield News-Sun

188

DENNIS DRAUGHON, Scranton Times

REX BABIN, Sacramento Bee

JIM MORIN
Miami Herald

Dick Cheney

Despite his dry and sometimes brooding personality, Vice President Cheney has proven to be a blessing to cartoonists with his insistence that Saddam Hussein was linked to the 9/11 attack, and his occasional use of colorful obscenities. Cheney's gruff, commanding style came into play in a conversation on the floor of the United States Senate with Senator Patrick Leahy (D - Vermont), where Cheney matter-of-factly told Leahy to "go %@&# himself." Cartoonists love this stuff. Of course if Cheney objects to these cartoons… he can go %@&# himself.

STEVE SACK, Minneapolis Star-Tribune

GREAT JOB, YOU KICKED BUTT.

VEEP DEBATE

PREZ DEBATE

STEVE KELLEY,
New Orleans
Times-Picayune

BILL DAY
Memphis
Commercial-Appeal

DOUG MARLETTE
Tallahassee Democrat

The WICKED WITCH of the WEST WING

DAVID HORSEY,
Seattle Post Intelligencer

MIKE KEEFE
Denver Post

CAMERON
CARDOW
Ottawa Citizen

193

JOHN KERRY IS A FRENCH-SPEAKING, FLIP-FLOPPING...

CHENEY

...TERRORIST-CODDLING, LYCRA-WEARING...

DAN
WASSERMAN
Boston Globe

...RESORT-HOPPING GIRLIE MAN!

NOW LET'S TALK ABOUT THE ISSUES

★⊙@#✕☠⚡@✳!

I SHOULD HAVE NEVER BOUGHT HER THAT "CHATTY CHENEY" DOLL.

DARYL CAGLE slate.com

194

JOE HELLER, Green Bay Press-Gazette

ROBERT ARIAIL, The State, SC

JOHN SHERFFIUS

DOUG MARLETTE
Tallahassee
Democrat

REX BABIN, Sacramento Bee

DREW SHENEMAN, Newark Star-Ledger

Paid for by the Committee to Re-Elect Bush/Cheney (If you know what's good for you)

M.e. COHEN

198 KEVIN KALLAUGHER, Baltimore Sun, CWS/CartoonArts International

PATRICK CHAPPATTE, International Herald-Tribune

CLAY JONES, Freelance-Star, VA

News Flash: Cheney Actually Didn't Say All Those Thing He Said

JEFF DANZIGER, CWS/CartoonArts International

Rippin' Kerry

John Kerry has been an icon on the American political scene ever since he returned from Vietnam and became the poster boy for the anti-war movement. He started with an appearance on the Dick Cavett show, followed by testimony before congress about the atrocities of war, and then a long career as a senator. Kerry took every opportunity to remind voters about his war record, while President Bush branded him a "flip-flopper." Cartoonists ran with the flip-flops, but not quite like some Americans, when a California internet company created John Kerry flip-flop sandals.

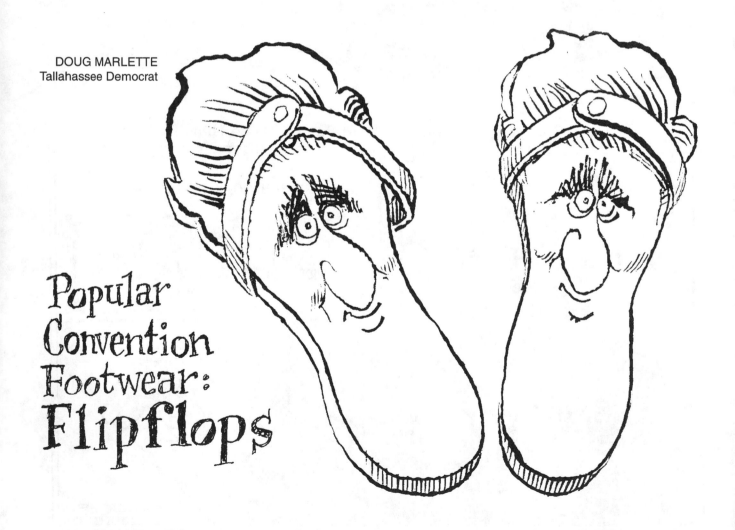

DOUG MARLETTE
Tallahassee Democrat

Popular Convention Footwear: Flipflops

BRIAN FAIRRINGTON
Arizona Republic

JIM MORIN,
Miami Herald

DAN WASSERMAN
Boston Globe

CAMERON CARDOW
Ottawa Citizen

DANA SUMMERS, Orlando Sentinel

ROBERT ARIAIL, The State, SC

JOE HELLER, Green Bay Press-Gazette

JOHN DEERING, Arkansas Democrat Gazette

JOE HELLER, Green Bay Press-Gazette

BRIAN FAIRRINGTON, Cagle Cartoons

STEVE KELLEY,
New Orleans Times Picayune

STEVE BREEN,
San Diego Union-Tribune

DARYL CAGLE
Slate.com

GARY MARKSTEIN, Milwaukee Journal-Sentinel

ERIC ALLIE, Pioneer Press (IL)

STEVE KELLEY, New Orleans Times Picayune

MIKE MIKULA

TAYLOR JONES, Tribune Media Services

VINCE O'FARRELL
Illawarra Mercury

MIKE KEEFE, Denver Post

208

SANDY HUFFAKER,
Cagle Cartoons

BRIAN FAIRRINGTON, Cagle Cartoons

209

Liberals vs. Conservatives

Perhaps no other time in America history has the country been as divided along ideological lines as in 2004, splitting the nation into hotly disputed "red" and "blue" states. Like two outlaw gunslingers marching slowly toward each other in an old western movie, people were facing down the opposition with increasing intolerance and hostility.

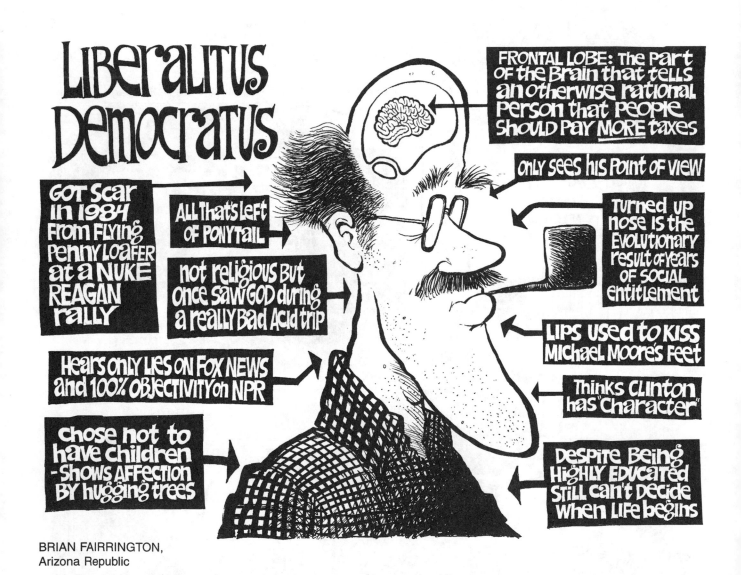

BRIAN FAIRRINGTON,
Arizona Republic

We're featuring these two cartoons as an example of America's divide because they generated more reader response to our web site than any other cartoons this year—close to ten thousand e-mails, divided evenly between supporters and detractors of each cartoon. Readers from both ideological camps were kind enough to write to cartoonists Cagle and Fairrington, praising their insights, while others wrote in with creative suggestions of things that the cartoonists could do with their anatomy, proving once again the beauty and irony of freedom of speech.

DARYL CAGLE, Slate.com

Dan Rather's Black Eye

Dan Rather, the anchor and managing editor of the *CBS Evening News*, went from covering the news to becoming the news faster that you can say "Alabama National Guard." The *60 Minutes* story, along with Rather's reputation, unraveled when it was discovered that CBS's documents showing that George W. Bush avoided fulfilling his commitment to the Alabama National Guard were forgeries.

Internet "bloggers" jumped on the story, studying details of the documents to prove that they were created in Microsoft Word and not on the typewriters that were available at the time Bush served in the National Guard.

Rather did his best impersonation of Richard Nixon by stonewalling until he was finally forced to admit his mistake.

TAYLOR JONES
Tribune Media Services

212

TIM MENEES
Pittsburgh Post-Gazette

MIKE LESTER
Rome News-Tribune, GA

DARYL CAGLE
Slate.com

JACK OHMAN, Portland Oregonian

JOHN
SHERFFIUS

DAN RATHER'S BLACK EYE

DOUG MARLETTE, Tribune Media Services

BILL SCHORR, AM New York

BRIAN FAIRRINGTON, Arizona Republic, Cagle Cartoons

216

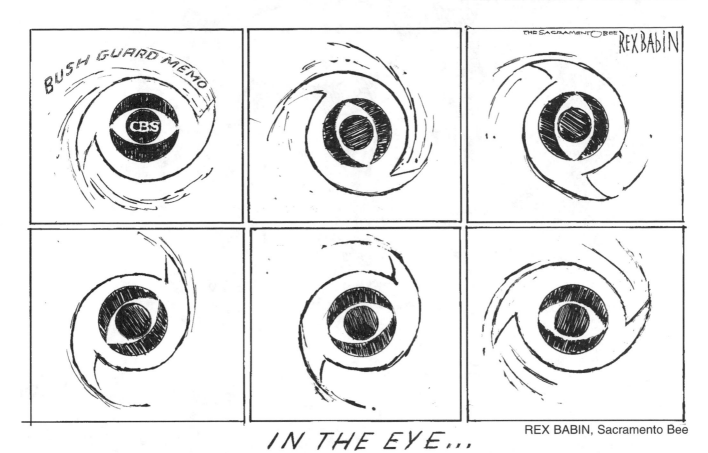

IN THE EYE...

REX BABIN, Sacramento Bee

LARRY WRIGHT, Detroit News

217

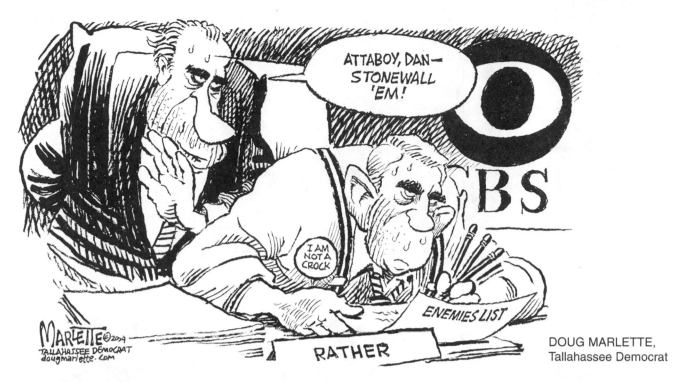

DOUG MARLETTE,
Tallahassee Democrat

CAL GRONDAHL, Utah Standard Examiner

KEN CATALINO, National/Freelance

JEFF PARKER, Florida Today

219

MIKE THOMPSON, Detroit Free-Press

CAMERON
CARDOW
Ottawa Citizen

GET READY BOYS—THIS IS THE MOST IMPORTANT ELECTION IN A **GENERATION**, AND YOUR **TWO MINUTES** OF FAME ARE COMIN' UP!

CORPORATE-OWNED

CORPORATE-OWNED

CORPORATE-OWNED

ABC   CBS   NBC

SANDY HUFFAKER, Cagle Cartoons

DAN RATHER'S BLACK EYE

SANDY HUFFAKER, Cagle Cartoons

VOTE **BUSH**   FOX INFOTAINMENT

FOR SALE

I ♥ O'REILLY

"RATHER HAS RUINED TRUST IN JOURNALISM—HE'S JUST <u>NOT</u> FAIR AND BALANCED!"

DICK LOCHER, Tribune Media Services

I'M NOT TOTALLY PREGNANT, AM I, DOCTOR?

OBY-GYNE

I DIDN'T TOTALLY DECEIVE YOU ON THE BUSH NATIONAL GUARD PAPERS, MR. RATHER.

©2004 CHICAGO TRIBUNE

BILL BURKETT

Bush Wins

George W. Bush pulled off what some political experts thought would be impossible: *He won,* getting more than three and a half million more votes than his opponent, John Kerry. The Republicans managed to expand their majorities in both the House and the Senate. Even worse for liberals, Bush would probably have an opportunity to stack the Supreme Court. Bush's political "architect," Karl Rove, had a strategy of bringing out conservative Christian voters by organizing votes to ban gay marriage across the nation. The nation was divided into red (Republican) and blue (Democratic) states—with lots of red in the middle, and not much blue on the coasts. Most voters said that "moral values" were the most important force in guiding their vote for Bush. Democrats were in a state of panic and disarray. Oh! The Humanity!

R.J. MATSON, Roll Call

ED STEIN
Rocky Mountain News

JAMES CASCIARI
Scripps Howard News Service

HENRY PAYNE
Detroit News

JOHN TREVER, Albuquerque Journal

DANA SUMMERS, Orlando Sentinel

MILT PRIGGEE

CHUCK ASAY
Colorado Springs Gazette

THE DECIDING FACTOR?
"MORAL VALUES"

voted for Bush because I'd rather remain unemployed with no health care than see two men get married

voted for Bush because I'd rather get drafted and die in that quagmire in Iraq than see two dudes holding hands

II voted for Bush because I'd rather lose ALL of my civil liberties than see two guys bein' all smoochy and crap!

SCOTT BATEMAN
National/Freelance

225

WALT HANDELSMAN, Newsday

GARY MARKSTEIN, Milwaukee Journal-Sentinel

DICK WRIGHT, Columbus Dispatch

CAMERON CARDOW, Ottawa Citizen

GARY MARKSTEIN, Milwaukee Journal-Sentinel

CHRIS BRITT, State Journal-Register, IL

227

ROB ROGERS, Pittsburgh Post-Gazette

BRUCE BEATTIE, Daytona Beach News-Journal

MIKE THOMPSON, Detroit Free Press

Four more years

JOHN SHERFFIUS

M. e. COHEN

VINCE O'FARRELL, Illawarra Mercury

229

Boston Red Sox

After an eighty six year losing streak, the Boston Red Sox finally won the 2004 world series against the St. Louis Cardinals, thereby overcoming Babe Ruth's infamous "Curse of the Bambino." Boston fans couldn't have been happier, and in a year filled with such ugly news, this was good news for everyone ... except Yankee fans.

MILT PRIGGEE

ROB ROGERS, Pittsburgh Post-Gazette

STEVE KELLEY, New Orleans Times-Picayune

BOB ENGLEHART, Hartford Courant

232

CLAY JONES
Freelance-Star, VA

JOHN DARKOW, Columbia Daily Tribune, MO

J.D. CROWE, Mobile Register

WALT HANDELSMAN, Newsday

SANDY HUFFAKER, Cagle Cartoons

DAN WASSERMAN, Boston Globe

on the web at www.ArtStudioSeven.com

combscartoons@yahoo.com © Paul Combs 2004

PAUL COMBS, Tampa Tribune

"BAD GOAT! BAD GOAT! DO YOU KNOW HOW LONG I'VE BEEN KEEPING THAT CURSE?!"

JOE HELLER, Green Bay Press-Gazette

MIKE LANE, Cagle Cartoons

Clinton Heart Surgery

President Clinton was again in the news when he underwent emergency bypass surgery to repair a blocked artery. He recovered in time to hit the campaign trail with John Kerry. Doctors told us that his heart attack was the result of a life-long diet of Big Macs, while cartoonists remembered Clinton's other appetites.

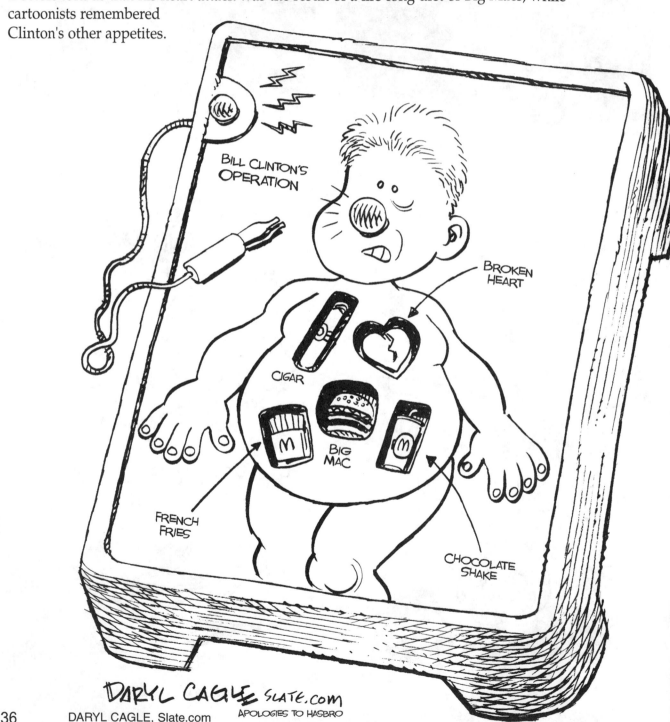

DARYL CAGLE, Slate.com

CAMERON
CARDOW
Ottawa Citizen

CHRIS BRITT, State Journal-Register

JOHN COLE, Durham Herald-Sun

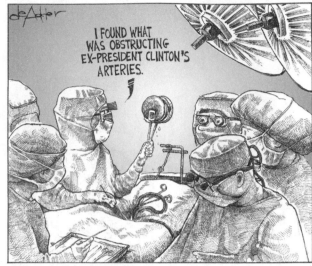

MICHAEL DEADDER, Halifax Daily News

STEVE BENSON, Arizona Republic

238

CAL GRONDAHL, Utah Standard Examiner

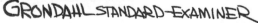

JIM DAY, Las Vegas Review Journal

STEVE KELLEY, New Orleans Times Picayune

The Middle East

The never-ending conflict between Israel and the Palestinians was marked by Yasser Arafat's death in 2004. His death brought new hope in Israel that there could be movement in the long stalled peace process. Violence flared regularly throughout the year with bombs on buses and military incursions into the occupied territories. Israeli Prime Minister Ariel Sharon pushed a plan to withdraw from the West Bank and Gaza, while building a "security fence." As the Palestinians took every opportunity to strike out at the Israelis, Sharon conducted a campaign of assassinations successfully taking out many Palestinian terrorist leaders.

MATT DAVIES
Journal News, NY

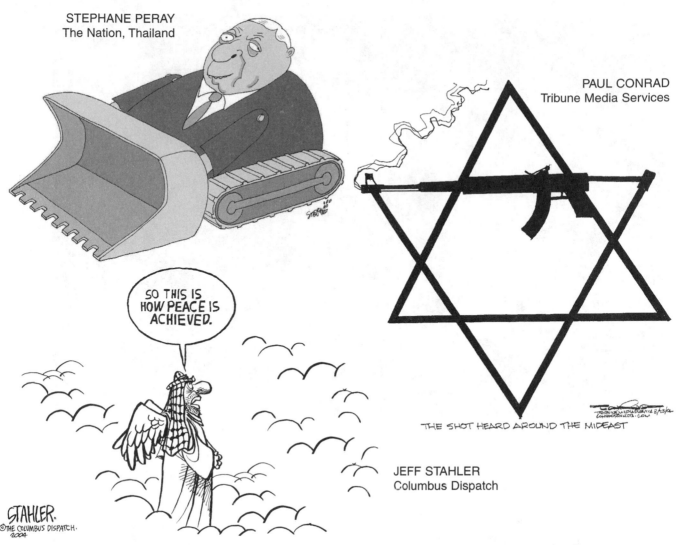

STEPHANE PERAY
The Nation, Thailand

PAUL CONRAD
Tribune Media Services

SO THIS IS HOW PEACE IS ACHIEVED.

THE SHOT HEARD AROUND THE MIDEAST

STAHLER.
© THE COLUMBUS DISPATCH.
2004

JEFF STAHLER
Columbus Dispatch

C.KELLY   THE TIMES·PICAYUNE
© 2 0 0 4

ARAFAT WIDOW MAY INHERIT BILLIONS

DON'T EVEN THINK ABOUT IT.

STEVE KELLY
New Orleans Times-Picayune

241

" NO...BUT, IT IS <u>YOUR</u> NEW HOMELAND..."

BILL SCHORR
AM New York

ALEN LAUZAN FALCON
The Clinic, Chile

YASSIR? THIS IS SHARON. I'M CALLING TO TELL YOU THAT BUSH WON. WHUPPED KERRY. KICKED HIS BUTT. BUSH HAS A MANDATE NOW AND HE'S GOING TO SPEND HIS POLITICAL CAPITAL. BOY! DID BUSH WIN, WIN, WIN. WHAT A WIN.

BIP... BIP...

HE HE HE!

OSMANI SIMANCA
Brazil

www.caglecartoons.com/espanol

STEVE SACK
Minneapolis
Star-Tribune

ROBERT ARIAIL
The State, SC

Views from Abroad

When foreign cartoonists looked at the USA in 2004, they didn't like what they saw.

Cartoonists around the world drew non-stop cartoons deploring President Bush, the war in Iraq, and anything American.

ARISTEDES ESTEBAN
HERNANDEZ GUERRERO
Cuba

JULIUS HANSEN
CWS/CartoonArts International
Denmark

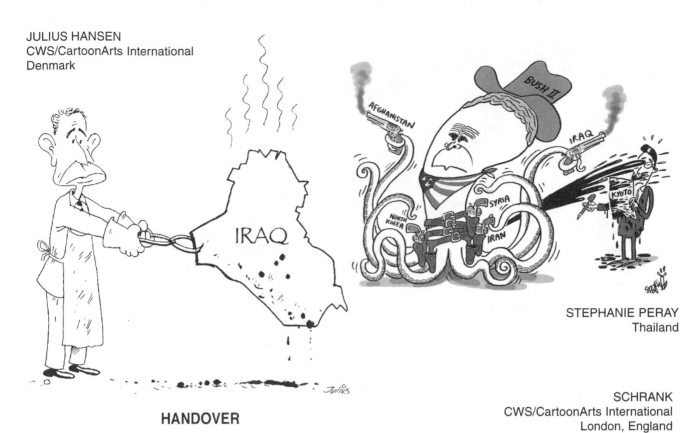

STEPHANIE PERAY
Thailand

SCHRANK
CWS/CartoonArts International
London, England

HANDOVER

STEMCELL HARDHEAD

SIMANCA OSMANI, Brazil

ROGELIO
NARANJO
Mexico

I SEE THE MONEY, BUT WHERE'S THE BRAINS?

BUDGET FOR DUMMIES
~~MY~~ BUSH
CAMPAIGN BUDGET

ARCADIO ESQUIVEL, Costa Rica

www.caglecartoons.com/espanol

GEORGE W. BUSH FOR PRESIDENT

MEXICO

SIMANCA OSMANI, Brazil

2004

IRAQ

SERGUEI, CWS/CartoonArts International, Paris, France

Cummings
CWS/CartoonArts
International
Winnipeg, Canada

..JAMMED..

BUSH

POLLS

CARTOONISTS & WRITERS SYNDICATE http://CartoonWeb.com

ALEN LAUZAN FALCON
Santiago, Chile

IRAQ

SAKAI
CWS/CartoonArts
International
Japan

BUSH

PANCHO
CWS/CartoonArts
International
Paris, France

DENG COY MIEL
CWS/CartoonArts International
Singapore

EXIT

WELL,
I'M LEAVING NOW,
I HAVE TO LEVEL
FALLUJA...

247

DOUMONT, CWS/CartoonArts International, Honduras

PARESH, CWS/CartoonArts International, India

GOMAA, CWS/CartoonArts International, Egypt

NICHOLSON, CWS/CartoonArts International, Australia

BATEUP, CWS/CartoonArts International, Australia

ZUDIN, CWS/CartoonArts International, Russia

BERTRAMS
CWS/CartoonArts, International
Netherlands

CARTOONISTS & WRITERS SYNDICATE http://CartoonWeb.com

CHEREPANOV, CWS/CartoonArts International, Russia

MEMECAN, CWS/CartoonArts International, Turkey

OLIVER SCHOPF
CWS/CartoonArts
International
Austria

Al Qaeda

Al Kerry

Code Orange

CORRIGAN, CWS/CartoonArts International, Canada

SUICIDE BOMBER

TERROR

STAVRO, CWS/CartoonArts International, Lebanon

MISSION ACCOMPLISHED-
HEADING HOME TO
FIGHT ELECTIONS...

KESHAV, CWS/CartoonArts International, India

FOR THE SAKE OF DEMOCRACY

AL-RAYIES, CWS/CartoonArts International, Saudi Arabia

GOD BLESS AMERICUH!

...and God help anybody else...!

ROY PETERSON
CWS/CartoonArts
International
Canada

251

FRANCISCO
CWS/CartoonArts
International
Philippines

IRAQ

COALITION TROOPS

GUREL
CWS/CartoonArts
International
Turkey

EMMERSON
CWS/CartoonArts
International
New Zealand

THE REAL STATE OF THE UNION

252

KICHKA, CWS/CartoonArts International, Israel

WONSOO, CWS/CartoonArts International, South Korea

TOM, CWS/CartoonArts International, Netherlands

KEMCHS
CWS/CartoonArts
International
Mexico

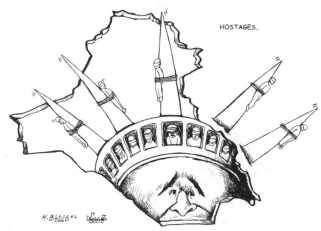

HOSTAGES..

BLEIBEL, CWS/CartoonArts International, Lebanon

LEAHY, CWS/CartoonArts International, Australia

PISMETROVIC, CWS/CartoonArts International, Austria

SLANE, CWS/CartoonArts International, New Zealand

FLIP-FLOP versus FLOP after FLOP after FLOP after FLO

TURNER, CWS/CartoonArts International, Ireland

MOIR, CWS/CartoonArts International, Australia

GUY BADO, WS/CartoonArts International, Canada

MOLINA
CWS/CartoonArts
International
Nicaragua

CARLUCHO, CWS/CartoonArts International, Mexico

255

RONNEN, CWS/CartoonArts International, Israel

PEEL, CWS/CartoonArts International, Norway

KIM SONG HENG, CWS/CartoonArts International, Singapore

GADO, CWS/CartoonArts International, Kenya

NIK KOWSAR
CWS/CartoonArts
International
Iran

AMMER, CWS/CartoonArts International, Austria

LAILSON, CWS/CartoonArts International, Brazil

THOMAS BOLDT
CWS/CartoonArts International
Canada

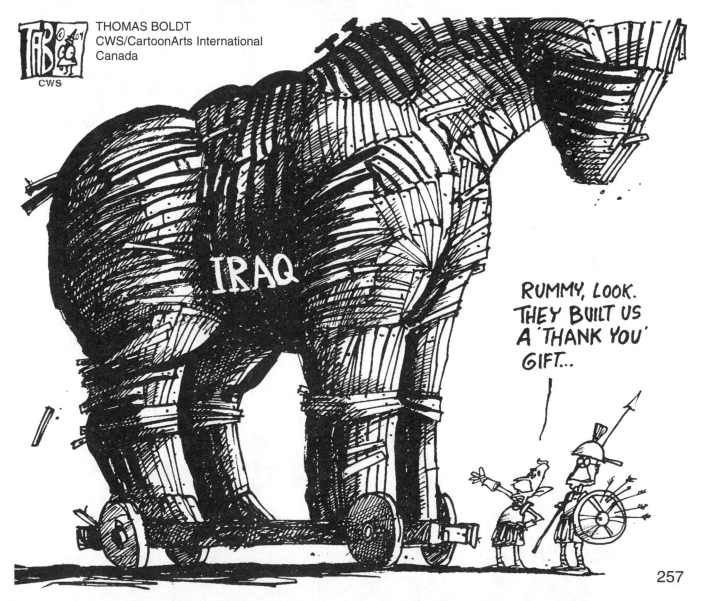

257

ZAPIRO, CWS/CartoonArts International, South Africa

BY HENRY MOORE

BY MICHAEL MOORE

CHRISTO
CWS/CartoonArts
International
Bulgaria

GRAFF, CWS/CartoonArts International, Norway

FAMOUS QUOTES THROUGHOUT HISTORY...

RODEWALT, CWS/CartoonArts International, Canada

BERTRAMS, CWS/CartoonArts International, Germany

HAJJAJ, CWS/CartoonArts International, Jordan

259

VEENENBOS, CWS/CartoonArts International, Austria

SAKURAI, CWS/CartoonArts International, Germany

LUOJIE, CWS/CartoonArts International, China

CLEMENT
CWS/CartoonArts
International
Canada

GABLE
CWS/CartoonArts
International
Canada

261

In Memorium

When celebrities pass away, cartoonists draw memorial cartoons. These are always the most popular cartoons with readers. The fan mail pours in whenever we draw celebrities greeted by Saint Peter at the Pearly Gates, as readers react to the cartoons with the warmth they felt for the celebrity who has passed on. This can be frustrating forcartoonists who take pride in throwing darts that bring down politicians, and who are complimented by their readers only when celebrities die. The most memorable cartoons of 2004 may be the ones drawn as memorials. Noteworthies who died in 2004 included actor Christopher Reeve, musician Ray Charles, actress Fay Wray, comedian Rodney Dangerfield, chef Julia Child, actor Marlon Brando, actress Janet Leigh and Captain Kangaroo.

JOHN SHERFFIUS

Mike Keefe THE DENVER POST 2004

LOOK! UP IN THE SKY!

CHRISTOPHER REEVE, 1952-2004

MIKE KEEFE
Denver Post

BOB ENGLEHART, Hartford Courant

MARSHALL RAMSEY, Clarion Ledger

BRUCE PLANTE, Chattanooga Times Free Press

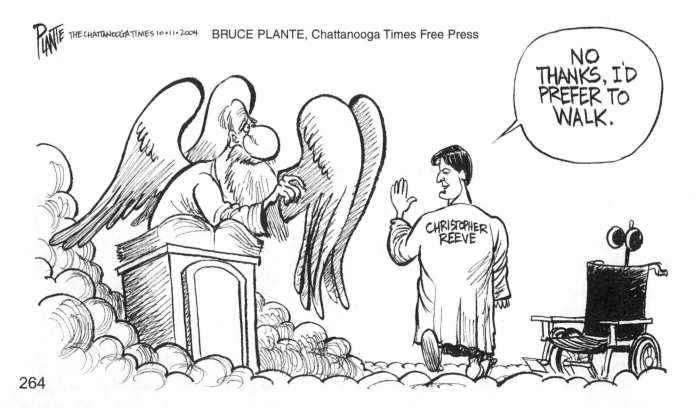

"HE WAS MY HERO..."

BILL SCHORR, AM New York

HE WAS THE MAN OF STEEL. HE HAD INCREDIBLE VISION. HE USED HIS POWERS TO SAVE PEOPLE. NOTHING COULD STOP HIM.

& BEFORE THAT, I THINK HE ACTED IN SOME SUPER-MAN MOVIES...

MATT DAVIES
Journal News, NY

TIM MENEES
Pittsburgh Post-Gazette

DOUG MARLETTE, Tallahassee Democrat

MARK STREETER, Savannah Morning News

266

RAY CHARLES
1930 – 2004

DWANE POWELL,
Raliegh News & Observer

BILL DAY, Memphis Commercial-Appeal

HENRY PAYNE, Detroit News

MARK STREETER, Savannah Morning News

JEFF STAHLER, Columbus Dispatch

Rodney Dangerfield 1921-2004

JIMMY MARGULIES, The Record, NJ

RODNEY DANGERFIELD
Nov. 22, 1921 - Oct. 5, 2004

VIC HARVILLE, Stephens Media Group

STEVE BENSON, Arizona Republic

MARK STREETER, Savannah Morning News

JEFF STAHLER, Columbus Dispatch

JEFF DANZIGER, CWS/CartoonArts International

CHIP BOK, Akron Beacon-Journal

MARK STREETER, Savannah Morning News

MARK STREETER, Savannah Morning News

271

PULITZER PRIZE

The Pulitzer Prize is the most prestigious award in the editorial cartooning profession. Cartoonists submit a portfolio of twenty cartoons for review by two committees at Columbia University. The 2004 winner was Matt Davies, of the Journal-News in New York, for this selection of cartoons that were published in 2003.

Matt pulled off a double coup by also winning the Herblock Award, a new prize named after the late cartoon legend, Herb Block, of the Washington Post. Matt submitted a dozen cartoons for the Herblock, from among the cartoons shown on these pages. Both the Herblock and Pulitzer come with $10,000 prizes, which were matched by Matt's newspaper. Congratulations to Matt!

"...THEY EXPANDED THE DEFINITION OF 'TERRORIST TIES'"...

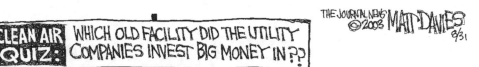

CLEAN AIR QUIZ: WHICH OLD FACILITY DID THE UTILITY COMPANIES INVEST BIG MONEY IN??

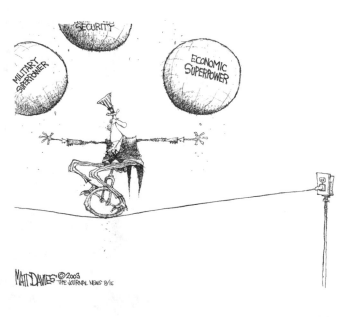

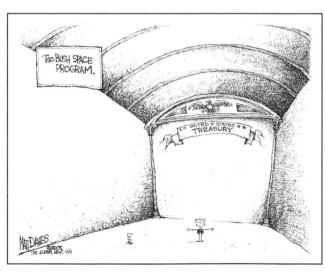

Index

To contact a cartoonist, visit our web site at **www.cagle.com/politicalcartoons** and click on a name. All of the cartoonists in this book have daily updated archives on our site, with links to the cartoonists' own web sites, their e-mail addresses, and contact information for their sales agents.